AURORA,
THEIR LAST UTOPIA

BY THE SAME AUTHOR

Early Portland: Stumptown Triumphant
Rival Townsites on the Willamette River, 1831–1854,
and Portland's victory in the battle to become
Oregon's metropolis.

Portland Names and Neighborhoods: Their Historic Origins
More than 950 street, school, and park names of
Portland, Oregon, with biographical and historical
information about their origins.

Portland Potpourri: Art, Fountains & Old Friends
Twenty-four historic and literary pieces, illustrated
with beautiful ink drawings and photographs, about
art work or landmarks easily seen in Portland or
about people with curious occupations.

Skidmore's Portland: His Fountain and Its Sculptor
Victorian Portland, from the 1850s to the 1880s, as
seen through the life of Stephen Skidmore. Includes
a biography of Olin Warner, the sculptor of
Portland's famous *Skidmore Fountain.*

We Claimed This Land: Portland's Pioneer Settlers
Biographies of the 212 pioneers who first owned the
land that is now Portland, Oregon. Many of these
first settlers acquired their land free under the
Donation Land Act.

THE COVER:
The painting reproduced on the cover shows an "O & C"
railroad train at the Aurora Colony Hotel, for a meal stop.
It is a watercolor by Oregon artist Clive Davies, based on
photographs taken in the 1870s.

AURORA, THEIR LAST UTOPIA

Oregon's Christian Commune, 1856–1883

by Eugene Edmund Snyder

Binford & Mort Publishing
Portland, Oregon

Aurora, Their Last Utopia
Oregon's Christian Commune, 1856–1883

Copyright © 1993 by Binford & Mort Publishing

Printed in the United States of America

Library of Congress Catalog Card Number: 93–74148

ISBN: 0-8323-0506-5 (hardcover)
ISBN: 0-8323-0507-3 (softcover)

First Edition 1993

Table of Contents

Chapter 1 The Christian Commune 1

Chapter 2 The Ruler: Dr. Keil 7

Chapter 3 Pious Separatists 11

Chapter 4 From Dissent to Harmony 15

Chapter 5 From Pittsburgh to Bethel 29

Chapter 6 From Bethel to Aurora 47

Chapter 7 Colony Days at Aurora 63

Chapter 8 The End of Utopia 97

Chapter 9 A Case History: The Forstner Saga 107

Postscript and Acknowledgments 133

Notes and References 135

Bibliography 137

Index 139

The Roads to Aurora

(Portland to Aurora, about 25 miles)

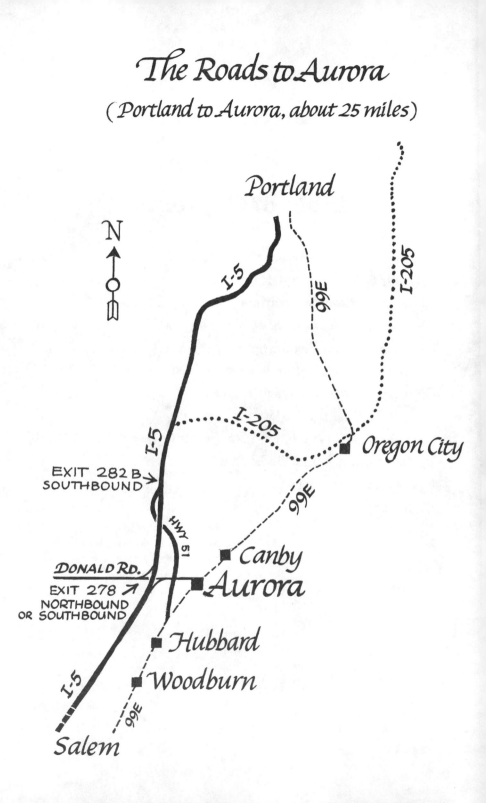

Chapter 1

The Christian Commune

Thirty minutes south of Portland and just off Interstate Highway 5 is Aurora, now a quaint community of antique shops but in the nineteenth century the site of Oregon's most famous communal utopia. Its history is a piece of Americana and part of the story of our western frontier. Aurora has been declared a National Historic District.

The Aurora Colony was established by pioneers who came from Missouri over the Oregon Trail in 1855. It was a long five-month journey. They went first to Willapa Bay in southwestern Washington, but that seaside location didn't suit them. It was too isolated from other early settlements, most of which were in the fertile Willamette Valley. So they moved to the Aurora site in the spring of 1856.

Aurora was a "colony" in that it was an offshoot of a similar community at Bethel, Missouri. There were 650 people at Bethel just before the emigration to Oregon. Thirty-five wagons with about 150 pioneers left in 1855 to establish the west-coast branch. A larger train of 42 wagons brought about 250 more people from Bethel to Aurora in 1863. More came in wagon trains in 1865 and 1867, and others came by ship, either around Cape Horn or via the Isthmus of Panama. By 1867, the population at

Aurora was larger than that remaining at the parent Bethel.

Oregon's Aurora Colony is often called a "German Christian Communist" society. That gives some idea of its character. but those words need to be defined. A better word than "German" might be "Germanic" because in the late eighteenth and early nineteenth centuries, when the Aurorans or their forebears left the Fatherland, there was no "Germany" as a political entity. That area was divided among many dukedoms, principalities, and kingdoms...as many as 300 independent units, some of them very small. The inhabitants thought of themselves as Swabians, Bavarians, Hessians, Prussians, etc. Their languages were Germanic, but they spoke different dialects. Only in 1870, under the unifying force of Prussia's Bismarck, did Germany become a national political state. But the Aurorans, or their ancestors, had left Europe long before that. Most of them emigrated during the Napoleonic upheavals and were in America by 1817. The majority were from the Swabian kingdom of Württemberg; others were from Bavaria, Baden, and northern Switzerland. They had settled originally in Pennsylvania, later moving to Bethel. By the time they reached Aurora, they were speaking "Pennsylvania Dutch," which is a mixture of the Swabian dialect, plus some Bavarian, Swiss German, and English. (It is erroneously called "Dutch" because, in German, the word for "German" is "deutsch." "Pennsylvania deutsch" came to be called "Pennsylvania Dutch.")

The Aurorans were Christian in their attempt to live the life implied or commanded by Jesus—humble, peaceful, non-materialist. Those aspects of Jesus' teachings might be called "first-century Christianity" or "Early Christianity." Another ingredient in their theology, as preached during their beginnings in Pennsylvania, described life on earth as a marking-time period while waiting for Christ's second coming, which they expected imminently. That tenet was less prominent by the time they reached Aurora, perhaps because the glorious event continually defied prediction or because they became preoccupied in building a village in the wilderness and enjoying the small pleasures of daily living. They were craftsmen who found fulfillment in the creative work of artisans. They also enjoyed music and—in moderation—their sweet wine.

The Aurorans were not affiliated with any religious denomination. Indeed, one of the beliefs which had been responsible for their ancestors' leaving their European homeland was that an individual needed no priest or cleric as an intermediary between himself and God. God's Holy Spirit, available to every person, was the all-sufficient link. This had set them apart from their Swabian and Bavarian neighbors, who were predominantly Lutheran or Roman Catholic.

What about "communist"? This word needs to be used with care in relation to the Aurora Colony. It may suggest revolutionary political activity based on Marxist slogans and ideology. One could hardly find an image less applicable to Aurora. The Aurorans were pacifistic and non-political. Some features of their society were communal, but they certainly were not Marxists. In fact, Karl Marx, born in 1818, might have been quite unknown to them. Long before his "Communist Manifesto" was published in 1848, the economic and social bases of the Aurora Colony had already been formed at preceding societies in Pennsylvania.

At Aurora, the colony leader owned some real estate and buildings in his own name, as a matter of practical convenience. And each member had been required, at the time of joining the Bethel community, to turn in all his cash to the common treasury. Colonists did not often use money in daily affairs; they contributed products to a common storehouse from which they withdrew what they needed. But some members did own real estate, and each family had its own house. Thus there was a mixture of common and private ownership. For Aurora, "communal" is a better word than "communist."

So, "a Germanic communal society based on early Christianity" would be a good description of the Aurora Colony.

Aurora was similar in some ways to dozens of other communal societies in America in the nineteenth century. For example, "Harmony" in Pennsylvania, "Zoar" in Ohio, and "Amana" in Iowa each combined the Germanic and pietistic Christian characteristics of Aurora but with different emphases according to the personalities and objectives of their leaders. And there were other communes built not on Christian theology but on secular precepts, such as romantic notions of an assumed nobility in human nature. Most were idealistic, utopian, and (compared with Aurora's 26 years of existence) short-lived.

Aurora had fewer peculiarities than most American communes. The Aurorans dressed like other rural Oregonians of the day. Unlike some communes, at Aurora the family was the basic social unit, and children were raised in the homes of their parents. The importance of the family was especially strengthened because it was part of their paternalistic theological hierarchy: a chain of command, so to speak, extending from family members to the *pater familias*, then to the leader of the Colony, and then to God the Father.

The Aurorans were less separated from "the world" than members of other communal societies. They had many interactions with their neighbors. They had a restaurant concession at the state fair; their hotel was a favorite resort, with a dining room that was famous; their park was rented to groups for picnics; and they had an excellent band which played in the region's towns and cities. Their communalism was not rigid; individual members could sell fruit and other products to the public to acquire a little private pocket money. Tobacco was not banned; some of the men smoked cigars or pipes. They made their own wine.

On the other hand, some of their practices set them apart from their neighbors. One was their cleanliness, often noted approvingly by visitors. Another was their plainness. They emphasized utility and had little interest in adornment or frills. In their houses, a concession to appearance might be an occasional hand-woven rug. Sometimes a father, with his non-communal pocket money, would buy a ribbon for a daughter's dress, but if they carried that too far, they would be admonished for yielding to "vanity." Some visitors found the environment rather drab.

Though Aurora's architecture and life-style tended to be plain and utilitarian, there was time occasionally for beauty and ornamentation, as shown by the Jacob Giesy house with its embellishments and trimmings going well beyond structural necessity.

Aurora had a good school, taught by well-trained German "professors," but there was little time for impractical "cultural" subjects. The curriculum was inclined towards reading, writing, and arithmetic.

The Aurorans' artistic impulse found its outlet in music, in handicrafts such as spinning, weaving, and quilting, in making furniture, and...in cooking!

Theory and practice in the Aurora Colony were laid down by their leader. It was he who founded the parent commune at Bethel, who led the 1855 wagon train to Oregon, and who was their temporal and spiritual guide and ruler: William Keil.

Chapter 2

The Ruler: Dr. Keil

An essential feature of a communal society is a strong leader. If "self" and self-interest are to be submerged into the common weal, the members will yield decision-making to that leader. Anything that sets him apart, that enshrines him in a cloak of awe, respect, or veneration will strengthen his effectiveness as an autocratic ruler.

He must be highly motivated and have a sense of "mission." Also, if he is to create the necessary religious fervor, he must be something of a "prophet"—at least, his followers must so regard him! He must have a magnetic personality and an inspiring message. Such an individual is likely to be somewhat eccentric. The leader of the Bethel and Aurora settlements exemplified all of those characteristics dramatically.

William Keil was born in 1812 in a village called Bleicherode, in central Germany. He was baptized in the Lutheran Church, the officially established church in that area. Bleicherode is near the town of Nordhausen, which is not far from the city of Erfurt. Erfurt, the site of one of Germany's oldest universities (established in 1392), is in Prussia, and the Keils would have spoken "hochdeutsch," that is, "high German." Well-educated Germans who met William Keil in later years censured his grammar, but at least his pronunciation (given the vanities of class-conscious humanity) would have tended to elevate him slightly above his followers in Pennsylvania and at Bethel, most of whom were from the more rustic South Germany and spoke some version of the Swabian dialect.

The young Keil had no formal education beyond elementary school. In those days, very few went to high schools, which were primarily "prep" schools for university. The great majority, at about the age of 14, became apprentices in a craft. William became a tailor.

In February 1836, he married Louisa Reiter, the event being solemnized in the Lutheran Church. Later that spring, the adventurous young couple (they were both 24 years old) emigrated to New York City. There, he worked as a tailor. But he was "restless" and "a dreamer and visionary." He had begun to read books on metaphysics. He was also interested in the theater and thought of becoming an actor—a propensity which must have been helpful in his later evangelical preaching. And he studied pharmacology, with the object, reportedly, of finding some universal panacea for all bodily ills! Clearly, he was something of a mystic. It was said that he performed cures with mysterious liquids he prepared from "secret formulas." Unfortunately, there is little documentary material covering this period of his life. Today's biographer must rely on secondary sources. Among these, however, there is universal agreement on his "imposing and magnetic personality." It is not unlikely that his hypnotic power of suggestion was a factor in the "miraculous" cures he achieved. William and Louisa's first child (Wilhelm, but known as "Willie") was born in New York City January 27, 1837. In 1838, the family moved to Pittsburgh, to live and work among the many German immigrants in western Pennsylvania. Their second son, August, was born there September 27, 1838. Mr. Keil continued his medicinal experiments and opened a drug store, though he had no formal training as an apothecary. But he did have an extensive knowledge of botany, and he grew herbs from which he prepared medicines that his contemporaries called "good and effective." He was self-taught, but results were what counted, and he achieved surprising cures with his "secret liquids." He began to call himself and to expect others to call him "Doctor Keil"—a courtesy title we will use henceforth. Among some of his German acquaintances he was known as "Der Hexen-Doktor," that is, the Doctor of Magic, the Magician, or the Wizard! Whether that appellation was intended as a compliment or a joke is unclear. In any case, such activities would not have been well received in the Lutheran Church, and we can assume that "Dr. Keil" was no longer a communicant.

But then occurred a decisive event which suddenly terminated Dr. Keil's somewhat bizarre vocation and determined his destiny. There was at that time in Pennsylvania an eloquent evangelist, William Nast, founder of an American denomination known as the "German Methodist Church." He came to Pittsburgh in 1838. Present at one of his revival meetings was Dr. Keil, who was "converted" to evangelical Methodism. He burned his secret formulas, denounced such things as diabolic, and, in 1839, became a preacher. But his connection with the Methodist Church didn't last long. He was too free a spirit, too strong-willed, to fit comfortably into any ecclesiastical hierarchy. The constrictions of creeds were intolerable for him. He said he would call himself nothing other than "Christian." But he continued as a free-lance evangelist, preaching in German communities in and around Pittsburgh.

His inspiration came entirely from the Gospels. Some observers who met Dr. Keil said the Bible was the only book he had ever read! That was an exaggeration, though it does emphasize the source of his ideas. He dwelt upon those verses that mentioned Jesus' disciples "having everything in common." But then he began to add another ingredient: separation from "the world." There were in America in the early nineteenth century many communal societies which had sought, out on the frontier, an Eden-like seclusion from worldly contamination where, in a Christian commune, they might create a sort of paradise on earth. Among them were the communities associated with George Rapp. His "Harmony" and "Economy" societies were well known in the U.S. and in Europe. In 1839, when Dr. Keil began to preach, Herr Rapp's village called "Economy" was located along the Ohio River just 18 miles north of Pittsburgh. Another group, ex-Rappites who had withdrawn from Economy because of disagreements about dogma, were living 10 miles farther downstream. It is certain that Dr. Keil was familiar with those societies.

Dr. Keil's message was one of Brotherhood and Comfort, to be attained by living and working together in a Christian commune separated from secular distractions, somewhere "out west." He found eager listeners and his followers soon numbered nearly a thousand—a testimony to his powerful personality and persuasive preaching. One reason for the enthusiastic reception was the national economic depression which began in 1837 and lasted several years. Another and perhaps more important reason was that there were living in western Pennsylvania many immigrants from German-speaking areas in Europe who had tried and liked communal living. Some 15 or 20 of the key men (and their families) in Dr. Keil's Bethel society were former Rappites. For that reason and because the Rapp communities were to some extent models for Bethel, we need to know something of their history and the motivations which brought George Rapp to America. After exploring those roots in Chapters 3 and 4, we will take up, in Chapter 5, the story of the migration of Dr. Keil and about 500 followers from Pittsburgh to Bethel, Missouri in 1844-45.

Chapter 3

Pious Separatists

Theologically speaking, the Aurora Colony, William Keil, and George Rapp were later manifestations of the Reformation and its aftermath. And that was one tumultuous chapter in Man's age-long search for the path to God. Until about 1500 (a convenient round number), that path had seemed rather well marked. The Roman Catholic Church was the traditional intermediary between Man and God. Church scholars like Augustine (354-420) and Aquinas (1225-1274) had erected a tightly-reasoned theological structure. Once the premises were accepted, all else followed neatly. No question, no troubling doubt could be raised for which there was not an answer in orthodox theology. The laity, of course, did not read the Bible. The Scriptures remained in beautifully illuminated volumes, written in calligraphic Latin by cloistered monks. The teachings of the Bible, as interpreted and amplified by Church tradition, were explained by the priests. For many centuries this arrangement worked to almost everyone's satisfaction, and the faithful passed peacefully from this world to the next, though there might have to be an uncomfortable stop-over in purgatory.

But then, as a result of some unsettling discoveries, the flat world became round, and on its other side were heathens who followed strange deities. The globular

earth was just another planet, it appeared, and the
universe became vast and seemingly less benign. The
theological edifice was shaken, but for the time being the
Church remained intact.

More disruptive was the printing press. Gutenberg
(1397-1468) perfected printing from type, and paper-
making techniques were developed which made paper
cheap enough for books to be printed economically. When
Luther (1483-1546) translated the Bible into German,
many copies were printed. In the 1500s, the Bible in
modern languages gradually became available and widely
read by the laity.

Now the Bible, particularly the New Testament with
its quotations from Jesus and St. Paul, is a powerful
document, as many people can personally testify and as
history plainly shows. The "conversion" of John Wesley
(1703-1791) is a striking example. The popular reading
of the Bible built up among pious laymen a desire to
return to the teachings and life-style of Jesus as
recorded in the Gospels. These dissidents grasped the
Bible as their "divinely inspired" guide. They saw no
need for a professional clergy.

Meanwhile, the violence and bloodshed of the Reformation had torn asunder the ecclesiastic establishment.
Northern Europe became Lutheran, or in the case of
England, "Church of England" (Anglican). In Germany,
some states became Lutheran, others Catholic, depend-
ing on the personal preference of the king or prince.
Whichever was the official church, everyone was expected,
and usually required, to belong to it. That church was
closely tied to the secular ruler—a bishop would crown
the king and the king would appoint the bishops. And
that official church was supported by compulsory taxes.

The dissidents ("nonconformists" they were called)
deplored all this. They saw society as too worldly, the
clergy as corrupt, the established church (whether

Catholic or Lutheran) as venal, and the pulpits filled with skeptics and rationalists! But when the "nonconformists" persisted in holding separate meetings and in staying away from regular church services, they came under attack from both the civil and clerical powers.

Württemburg was in the center of the noncomformist rebellion. The Swabians, some of them at least, seem to have been particularly susceptible to the appeals of simple pietistic "first-century" Christianity. But dissent was widespread. In Holland, Menno Simons (1492–1559) was a dissenter whose followers became the Mennonites. In Switzerland, there were famous reformers such as Zwingli (1484–1531) and Calvin (1509–1564). Lay preachers like George Rapp were a continuation of this long line of searchers for salvation through a personal "conversion" or encounter with God, attainable by reading the Bible.

Chapter 4

From Dissent to Harmony

George Rapp was born in 1757 at Iptingen, Württemberg, a village about 12 miles northwest of Stuttgart. He was a farmer, specializing in grape-growing, and also a weaver. He studied the Bible intensively, and he began to teach and preach in his home. He had not attended seminary nor been ordained, so he was very much outside the ecclesiastical hierarchy. At first, however, he remained in the established Lutheran state church; he had his son and daughter baptized there. He had begun preaching in 1787 when he was 30 years old and by 1793 about 300 families had become his followers. Most of them were from villages and towns within a radius of about 25 miles from his home. The number in his group continued to grow, and Herr Rapp withdrew from the official church. He and his followers became a congregation of nonconformists, denounced by their neighbors and the clergy as "separatists."

Some extreme nonconformists refused to pay church taxes (to support a church they didn't attend) or to serve in the king's army. Such rebels were often imprisoned. Herr Rapp advocated obeying the law, and he and his followers paid their taxes. Since he based all his teachings on Scripture, he probably was guided in this by a literal reading of the Biblical passage where Jesus, asked if the people should pay their taxes, said, "Render unto Caesar the things that are Caesar's."

But Herr Rapp and his congregation did not escape intolerance from their neighbors nor persecution from the established church. He was called before a church council to justify his separatism and to explain why he was not seen in church on Sunday. At this time, Herr Rapp was about 40 years old, a sturdily-built six-footer (at that time when the average height was much less than it is today), with flashing blue eyes and a stately stride. The scene in the councilroom must have been dramatic. His answer was that he had found "a better light," namely, Christ's Holy Spirit, with whom anyone could be in communion, so that rituals, sacraments, adn an ordained clergy were superfluous—an answer which could hardly have pleased his interrogators.

If one does not like his worldly milieu, he can do one of three things: (1) try to change it, which might mean revolt or rebellion; (2) adapt to it; that is, compromise; or (3) separate from it by immuring oneself in a cloistered monastery, emigrating, or retreating to a wilderness. The Rappites were too peace-loving to revolt and too firmly convinced to compromise, so they decided to emigrate. They said, "If we could find a land where religious toleration is enjoyed, we would wish to be there even if we might for a while have to live on roots."

It is not surprising that they chose the United States. Thousands of Wurttembergers and other Germans had already gone there, particularly to Pennsylvania, the territory granted to William Penn in 1581 by Charles II. It was the king himself who named it "Penn's Woods." William Penn was a Quaker who had personally endured some intolerance. He opened his territory to religious dissenters, and encouraged immigration from Germany. Some began arriving as early as 1683. Among many others, the United Brethren began arriving in 1735. By

1741, there were 100,000 Germans in Pennsylvania. Many, of course, did not come as separatists but remained Lutherans; they came for economic, not religious, reasons. All of this was well known to the pietists in Württemberg in the 1790s.

In 1803, the Rappites sold some of their properties, contributing the funds to Herr Rapp, who came to America to buy land. He was accompanied by his son, John, and by a Dr. Friedrich Conrad Haller. They sailed from Amsterdam on the ship *Canton*, arriving at Philadelphia October 7, 1803. At a site 26 miles north of Pittsburgh, they bought 4,500 acres, at $2.50 per acre. The next year, several hundred of his congregation arrived. The *Aurora* brought 300 from Amsterdam to Baltimore in July 1804. The *Atlantic* brought 269 to Philadelphia in September 1804, and the *Margaret* brought 270 later that month. The next year, on August 26th, the *Margaret* landed another group at Philadelphia. Hundreds more followed in later years.

On February 15, 1805, the Rappites gathered at their new home, which they named "Harmony," and formed a "Society in common." They all signed a contract with these provisions:

(1) Every member to give all money, property, and assets to the Society;

(2) Every member to obey the rules of the Society (in effect, the orders of "Father Rapp" as he had come to be called—he was now 48 years old);

(3) The Society (again, basically, Father Rapp) to provide members with all necessities of life in sickness and in health, to educate the children, and to look after the families of deceased members;

(4) Any member could withdraw at any time, in which case he would receive back the value of everything he had originally contributed, but without interest, and he would

make no demand for payment for his time or labor spent in the Society.

The members would be living in a theocracy, yielding their freedom of decision-making to their spiritual leader, who promised them total care for both body and soul. To us in the 1990s, when "individual freedom" has become a sacrosanct cliché, it might seem that they were giving up too much. But they had confidence in "Father Rapp," whom they revered as a prophet. Also, in the world at that time, there was very little "social security" anywhere. And they would be living among people whom they knew and liked and whose spiritual and cultural values they shared. Viewed in that perspective, it must have seemed a good bargain.

But after only a year at Harmony, the Rappites concluded that its site was not to their liking. For one thing, it was not on a navigable river, and river transportation was very important in those days. The Ohio River, from Pittsburgh on down to its confluence with the Mississippi, was the region's commercial artery. But Harmony was 12 miles from the Ohio River and 26 miles from Pittsburgh, long distances by wagon over unimproved roads.

Another disadvantage was that the soil around Harmony was not suitable for growing grapes. The Rappites were from one of Germany's most famous wine-making areas, and Father Rapp and many of his followers had owned vineyards, or were vine-dressers or wine-makers.

To find a better location, Herr Rapp wrote a memorial to President Jefferson asking for a large tract of more suitable land farther west. The memorial, written in 1805, was signed by all the members of the Harmony Society. It began with an eloquent explanation of the group's motivation in coming to the United States:

"Through the Grace of God and the enlightening help of the Holy Spirit, we decided

to follow the path of Piety, following the
words of Jesus. We formed a community in
which eventually were about 2,000 men [and
their families]. We were persecuted and
punished in many ways, for the sake of the
Faith which we perceived to be the Truth.
Therefore, it was necessary for us to look for a
place where there is liberty of conscience and
where we could practice, without inter-
ference, the religion of the Spirit of Jesus."

After that introduction, Father Rapp described the
economic base of the Society, and its needs. He wrote that
his Society consisted of "tradesmen, farmers, and chiefly
cultivators of the vine, which last occupation they con-
template as their primary object." He added, in his Germanic English with some personalized spelling, "They
know to plant and prepare Hemp and flax, having good
weavers among them, so they are intended to erect, too, a
Linen manufactory." But growing grapes and making wine
were to be their principal vocation. However, their property
at Harmony was "too small, too broken & too cold for to
raise vine...the culture of vine requires a peculiar climate
and soil." He went on to ask the federal government to grant
them 30,000 acres "in the western country," for which "the
whole Society does bind themselves to pay." A decade passed
before the Society moved to a large new site in Indiana.
Meanwhile, they worked industriously to develop Harmony.
They planted thousands of fruit trees and some vineyards
(apparently, the land was not utterly hopeless for that
purpose) and built 130 buildings, including two distilleries,
grist mills, saw mills, a brick kiln, a brewery, a nail factory,
and barns for horses and 3,000 sheep.

Amidst all this energetic material accomplishment,
Father Rapp reminded members daily that "the end is
near," that Christ's second coming was imminent, and

that they should live in holiness. In 1807, he took a step towards making the Society even more angelic: he began to preach celibacy! At an emotional revival meeting, the Society voted to adopt celibacy as its ideal. Those who were single would remain so; those already married would live celibate lives henceforth. For people living in the sensual 1990s, this might be hard to understand. However, there are passages in the New Testament which suggest that sexual intercourse could be regarded as a frailty, permissible only because of our weaknesses and imperfections. In Christian tradition, the celibate state has often been considered the most holy and the most pleasing to God. Certain Bible verses can be found which might be interpreted to support that view. For example:

> St. Paul (I Cor 7:7-8). It is best to remain unmarried if you can; but not everyone has this gift.

> St. Paul (I Cor 7:27). If you are not married, the best is to remain so; but if you do marry you are not thereby committing a sin.

> St. Paul (I Cor 7:29). The time is short; so those that are married should live as though they were not married.

> St. Paul (I Cor 7:32-34). He that is unmarried careth for the things that belong to the Lord, how he may please the Lord; but he that is married careth for the things of the world, how he may please his wife.

> Jesus (Matt 19:10-12). To be celibate is a gift, which is not given to everyone.

> Jesus (Matt 22:30). In the resurrection, they neither marry nor are given in marriage, but are as the angels in heaven.

Father Rapp—he already had two children—must have agonized over such Bible passages. He took every sentence in the Bible as the literal Word of God. His goal was to achieve the highest holiness conceivable; he spoke of presenting himself and his flock as an acceptable gift to the Lord. And he was confident that Christ's second coming would occur in his own lifetime. So, in zealous righteousness, he submitted his new revelation to the congregation in an emotional sermon ending, perhaps, with the injunction, "Mortify the Flesh!" Considering the greater the sacrifice the greater the blessing, the greater the agony the greater the ecstasy, the congregation all said, "Amen!" Or most of them did. A few did leave the Society at that time. Some others disliked the new rule, but because of Father Rapp's charismatic power and authority, and the members' veneration for him, the opposition remained latent for the time being. But the seeds of schism were sown, as we shall see.

The new rule of celibacy was adopted as their policy and ideal, but it was not enforced absolutely. Some married couples continued producing children. However, due partly to social pressures but mostly to their agreeing with the theology, the Society's birth rate declined steeply and eventually approached zero.

Father Rapp ceased to perform or allow new marriages; young people could not marry and still remain full members of the Society. But population at Harmony didn't decline, and even increased, because additional Rappites arrived from Württemberg.

At about the same time the Harmonists adopted celibacy, they also voted to ban tobacco—another step towards holiness. As to alcohol, their attitude was more complex. They made and drank wine; it would have been difficult for literalists to ignore the many Scriptural references to wine-drinking. Indeed, the Bible makes it clear, in verses such as Luke 7:34, that Jesus Himself drank wine. But "hard liquor" was something else, and the Harmonists strictly abstained from that. Even so, they had distilleries and produced and sold much whisky. Their "Harmony" brand was famous for its excellence. (But surely the distillery crew had to monitor the product for quality control? Perhaps they had a special dispensation from Father Rapp allowing them to sniff the distillate and to swish it around the tongue, to check the taste, but not to swallow it.)

In 1815, the whole community moved to Indiana. Two years before that, Father Rapp had sent his assistant, Frederick Reichert, to look for a suitable site farther west. He found 20,000 acres of federal land, which he acquired under the Homestead Act, and he bought 10,000 adjoining acres from private owners. In 1814, an advance party had begun to clear the land. The Society sold all the property and buildings at Harmony for $100,000 (a sum which would have to be multiplied by at least 20 to equal the diminished dollars of the 1990s), and in the spring of 1815 the Harmonists, numbering by then about 800, floated down the Ohio River to Indiana.

Their new site was on the bank of the Wabash River, about 25 miles above its confluence with the Ohio, so they had good water transport. They went to work vigorously to build another town, which they named "New Harmony." The soil was rich and they planted vineyards. They built a large brick mansion for Father Rapp and brick or frame two-story houses for each family. Every family property was well fenced and had its own vegetable and flower garden.

There were three-story dormitory buildings for the single members. And they built a large and elegant church, described by a visitor in these words: "I can scarcely imagine myself to be in the wilds of Indiana...while passing through the long and resounding aisles and surveying the stately colonnades of this church."[1] There were also, of course, the factories and shops which made the community almost self-sufficient and provided many products to sell: buildings for spinning, weaving, flour milling, a steam sawmill, a machine shop, wine-presses, distilleries, and a brewery.

More and more of the Society's affairs were left to Fred Reichert, whom Father Rapp legally adopted as his son. He did that not only, perhaps, so much for filial affection (he already had a real son) but to simplify the eventual transfer of title to the property; Fred was his chosen heir to lead the Society. Fred managed the day-to-day affairs, leaving Father Rapp, now in his 60's, to look after spiritual and devotional matters.

Father Rapp required "auricular confession" (that is, confession spoken directly to him) if any member had a quarrel or misunderstanding or had broken a Commandment or transgressed in any way. Such a sinner was expected to come to Father Rapp before bedtime and confess verbally. This, again, was based on certain Biblical passages, for example:

> "Let not the sun go down upon your wrath." (Eph. 4:26)

> "Confess your faults one to another...that ye may be healed." (James 5:16)

> "If we confess our sins, God is faithful and just to forgive us our sins." (I John 1:9)

Father Rapp was trying to lead his people to a holiness suitable for heaven (where they expected to be very soon), but imperfect mankind (and that generic word *does* embrace women) are prone to selfishness, envy, pride, carnal excesses, and to breaking the Decalogue in many other ways. To achieve angelic holiness was a difficult assignment, but philosophers would probably agree that the ideal, though by definition almost impossible to achieve, should guide behavior and practice.

The years on the Wabash were prosperous. Under Fred's management, the Society sold its goods up and down the Ohio and Mississippi rivers. Amidst the privations and the primitive log cabins of the backwoodsy frontier, New Harmony was like an oasis of European culture—neat, clean, comfortable, with singing, a band playing daily, and flowers. And (to paraphrase the Indiana state song) the moonlight shone beautifully along the Wabash, the scent of new-mown hay came from the fields, and the candlelight gleamed through the sycamores. Despite all this, the New Harmonists were not happy there. Some of them had malaria—it was swampy along that riverbank. Their few rustic neighbors did not understand them and were even somewhat hostile—though also envious! And the market for their products had less potential than the more developed area around Pittsburgh which they had left. Also, there, they had been near thousands of other European immigrants, even though somewhat sequestered from them. So they decided to return to western Pennsylvania.

In 1824, Father Rapp sold New Harmony to the only buyer he could find—Robert Owen, a British "social engineer" who established there a short-lived secular commune. The Harmonists received about $150,000 for their 30,000 acres, the town, and ten years of hard labor—much less than the replacement value, but enough to enable them to move back to Pennsylvannia and buy a new site there.

When Owens' group moved into the houses so carefully built by the Harmony carpenters, they found this inscription written in one of them:

> On the 24th of May 1824 we have departed. Lord, with thy great help and goodness, protect us in body and soul.[2]

The move back upstream, during 1824-25, was simplified because the Harmony mechanics had built a steamboat in 1824. This was one of the earliest steamboats on the Ohio River, and it showed that those artisans could adapt their traditional skills to new inventions and techniques. Their steamboat was a pride and joy to them.

Their new site was 13 miles below Pittsburgh, on the bank of the Ohio River, with good water transport and a populous urban market for their products. There they went to work building a THIRD complete town. They named it "Economy," not to suggest frugality but efficient management and organization of production. "Economy" was a subtle change from "Harmony," showing, perhaps, the growing ascendancy, in secular matters, of Frederick Reichert Rapp over Father Rapp. The adopted son, intelligent and practical, was the Society's manager and representative in business relations with the outside world. During their days along the Wabash, he had been a member of the Indiana state legislature, a worldly involvement indeed.

In 1832, a schism split the Economists. The previous autumn, one Bernard Müller (alias Count Leon) had arrived at Economy from Germany. With him were a few followers, a seemingly courtly entourage. He claimed to be a "prophet," and he sent envoys ahead to impress the Economists and prepare the way for "the anointed one," as he called himself. He and his retinue arrived with great fanfare.

According to some accounts, Father Rapp thought Herr Müller might be the "Messiah!" We must remember that Father Rapp was convinced that he would not die before Christ's return to earth. He was now 74 years old and possibly becoming a little anxious. The Count had not been at Economy long, however, before Father Rapp recognized his error in attributing anything divine to the impostor, and asked him to leave. But the Count declined to leave; he and his retinue continued living in, and on, Economy. Winter was approaching, and Father Rapp was too charitable to eject forcibly the flamboyant fakes. The rule of the Society was never to turn away anyone who came asking for food or shelter.

If the prosperous and would-be-holy Economy community might be likened to the Garden of Eden, the bogus Count clearly had some of the characteristics of the Serpent. He detected, in talking with the members, some latent dissatisfaction, and he began to preach a less austere life—more luxurious clothing, better food, more comforts, and an end to celibacy. Many of the members, especially the younger ones, listened to him. The Count claimed not only that he was a "prophet" but that he could transmute base metal into gold! Perhaps, with a little sleight-of-hand, he substituted a gold coin for a copper penny, deluding some of the more credulous Economists. Count Leon, besides being a charlatan, must have been a consummate actor.

The Leonists became more insistent, and finally Father Rapp felt obliged to ask for a vote of confidence. Of the 750 members at that time, 250 voted for Count Leon. Father Rapp quoted an appropriate Bible passage (Revelation 12:4) to describe this defection:

> The tail of the serpent [an allegorical reference to Satan] drew the third part of the stars of heaven, and did cast them to earth.

In the spring of 1832, after some bickering, 176 members of the Economy society withdrew with Count Leon. Evidently, of the 250 who originally voted for Count Leon, 74 had more sober second thoughts, if not about the proposed liberalized life-style, at least about the Count. Father Rapp and the loyal Economists paid the seceders $105,000, representing their share of the Society's assets.

They used $22,000 to buy 800 acres on the bank of the Ohio River about eight miles downstream from Economy. The landowner from whom they bought the tract was Stephen Phillips, whom they honored by naming their new site Phillipsburg—appropriate, perhaps, but less inspirational than "Harmony." There they set to work building what was for most of them a FOURTH complete town. During their first month at Phillipsburg, even before the carpentry work was well underway, 20 young men and women were united in marriage—something that would not have been allowed if they had remained at Economy. (Those of us who are descended from those unions must be grateful for the schism?)

After 12 months at Phillipsburg, the Leonists had built 50 houses, a hotel, some shops, and a church. But they had spent most of their money and had no income. The Count, in these practical matters, was a poor manager—much less skillful than in demagoguery. Attempts to extort more money from Economy were resisted. In the summer of 1833, the Count and his original retinue fled in a boat down the Ohio River (according to some accounts, absconding with what was left in the treasury). He died later that year in Louisiana, of cholera.

The Phillipsburg society was dissolved in August 1833. Its assets were divided among the members, and those communal "utopians" were left to make their own individual ways, adrift in secular society. After the womb-like care and prescribed routine of Harmony and Economy, "the world" must have seemed to them like a jungle.

We have followed the Rappite saga in some detail because those societies were models for Dr. Keil's Bethel and Aurora "utopias" and because some of his leading members had formerly been at Harmony, Economy, and Phillipsburg. In the area around Pittsburgh, where Dr.

Keil preached and found his followers, there were a number of unattached "utopians" who were ready to listen to him and who brought with them considerable experience in communal building and living.

To conclude the story of Father Rapp, we will note that Frederick Reichert Rapp, his chosen heir, died in 1834 as a result of injuries when a tree fell on him. The entire management of Economy devolved upon Father Rapp, who was then 77 years old.

Father Rapp died in 1847, aged 90. Not long before his death, when he was gravely ill, he said, "If I did not know that the dear Lord meant that I should present you all to Him, I would think that my last moments had come."[3] Soon it became clear even to him that he was dying, and he called into his room, one by one, every member of the Economy Society, gave each his blessing and charged them to remain true to the ideals he had taught. The surviving loyal Economists were well off in their old age, but, with no new members, the Society gradually faded away.

The site of Economy is now the town of Ambridge, and the site of Phillipsburg is now Monaca.

Chapter 5

From Pittsburgh to Bethel

It was in 1838, four years after the Count Leon affair, that the Keils moved from their New York City tailor shop to Pittsburgh.

Dr. Keil was for a short time during 1839-40 a Methodist preacher, though his connection with the church was unofficial. Then, as we saw in Chapter 2, he became an independent evangelist. It is highly probable that he visited Father Rapp, who was still living nearby at Economy. Certainly, he knew of him, because many of Dr. Keil's disciples were among the disillusioned former Rappites at Phillipsburg. Other important converts included the Swiss-German family of Andrew Giesy, whose farm was at Sewickley, nine miles downstream from Pittsburgh. Andrew, his wife, and their family followed Dr. Keil to Bethel, and several of their 14 children became key members.

One ingredient in Dr. Keil's message was "separation from the world," to be achieved by living in a Christian commune out on the sparsely-settled frontier. He understood, as had Father Rapp, the difficulty of living a life of holiness if one is surrounded by worldly distractions and temptations. Many among Dr. Keil's adherents expressed a willingness to follow him "into the wilderness." So he sent three of his congregation as agents to find a suitable tract "out west." These three were Adam Schuele, David

Wagner, and Christian Presser. Schuele and Wagner were former Rappites who had withdrawn from Economy with Count Leon; Dr. Keil recruited them from among the survivors at Phillipsburg.

In the spring of 1843, the three scouts went to St. Louis, then a good base from which to search for undeveloped western acreage. By that time, the trip there from Pittsburgh had become relatively easy.

During the nineteen years since the New Harmony craftsmen had built their early steamboat in 1824, population had grown, villages had become towns, and there were now many steamboats on the Ohio River. Helping us to visualize the scene at Pittsburgh and the river traffic at that time are some passages in the book, *American Notes*, by Charles Dickens, who toured the U.S. in 1842. That spring, he and his wife made exactly the same journey the three scouts would make 12 months later. As we read the great English novelist's description of that trip, we must remember that he was also a humorist.

> "Pittsburgh is like Birmingham in England, at least its townspeople say so.... It certainly has a great quantity of smoke hanging about it, and is famous for its iron-works.... It is very beautifully situated on the Allegheny River...and the villas of the wealthier citizens sprinkled about the high grounds in the neighborhood are pretty enough. We lodged at a most excellent hotel and were admirably served.... Our next point was Cincinnati; and as this was a steamboat journey, and western steamboats usually blow up one or two a week...it was advisable to collect opinions in reference to the comparative safety of the vessels bound that way, then lying in the river. One called the *Messenger* was the best recommended."

Mr. and Mrs. Dickens stayed three days in Pittsburgh, and went aboard the *Messenger* at noon on Friday, April 1, 1842.

"The *Messenger* was one among a crowd of high-pressure steamboats, clustered together by a wharf-side.... She had some forty passengers on board, exclusive of the poorer persons on the lower deck.... We had, for ourselves, a tiny stateroom with two berths in it. [Their stateroom was near the stern of the vessel.] We had been a great many times very gravely recommended to keep as far aft as possible, 'because the steamboats generally blow up forward.' Nor was this an unnecessary caution, as the occurrence and circumstances of more than one such fatality during our stay sufficiently testified.... We are to be on board the *Messenger* three days, arriving at Cincinnati (barring accidents) on Monday morning."

The Ohio was "a fine broad river.... Occasionally, we stop for a few minutes, maybe to take in wood, maybe for passengers, at some small town or village...but the banks are for the most part deep solitudes, overgrown with trees.... For miles, and miles, and miles, these solitudes are unbroken by any sign of human life or trace of human footstep; nor is anything seen to move about them but the blue jay.... At lengthened intervals a log cabin, with its little space of cleared land about it.... Sometimes the ground is only just now cleared, the felled trees lying yet upon the soil and the log-house only this morning begun. As we pass this clearing, the settler leans upon his axe...and looks wistfully at the

people from the world.... Evening slowly
steals upon the landscape...when we stop to
set some emigrants ashore."

This description of the bleak desolation between the
few towns makes it easier for us to understand why the
Rappites at New Harmony, two decades *before* the
Dickens' trip, felt isolated out on the bank of the Wabash
River.

Mr. Dickens continued:

"Leaving Cincinnati at eleven o'clock in the
forenoon, we embarked for Louisville in the
Pike steamboat, which, carrying the mails,
was a packet of a much better class than that
in which we had come from Pittsburgh....
This day's journey...brought us at midnight
to Louisville. We slept at the Galt House, a
splendid hotel; and were as handsomely lodged
as though we had been in Paris."

At Louisville, they boarded another steamboat, the
Fulton, which took them to St. Louis—two days to Cairo,
Illinois, where the Ohio River joins the Mississippi, and
another two days upstream against the current of the
Mississippi River to St. Louis. The spring freshet had
swollen the river, in both size and velocity. Here is Mr.
Dickens' description of "the big muddy" at that time in
1842:

"What words shall describe the Mississippi
...an enormous ditch, sometimes two or three
miles wide, running liquid mud, six miles an
hour; its strong and frothy current choked
and obstructed everywhere by huge logs and
whole trees.... For two days we toiled up this
foul stream, striking constantly against the

floating timber or stopping to avoid snags. The look-out stationed in the head of the boat knows by the ripple of the water if any great impediment be near at hand, and rings a bell, which is the signal for the engine to be stopped...always at night this bell has work to do, and after every ring, there comes a blow which renders it no easy matter to remain in bed."

Their trip from Pittsburgh to St. Louis took about eight days, but they spent two nights ashore and also did some sight-seeing. Dr. Keil's three scouts, when they traveled the same route 12 months later, could probably have made it in five or six days. In any case, their trip would have been very much the same.

The scouts found a tract which suited them in Shelby County, Missouri. It comprised four sections of government land (a total of 2,560 acres) located 45 miles by wagon road from the Mississippi River port of Hannibal, Missouri. Hannibal is 110 miles above St. Louis and 270 miles upstream from Cairo. (Those antique names bestowed on townsites along the Mississippi River—Alexandria, Hannibal, Herculaneum, Thebes, Cairo, Memphis—gave "the big muddy" a touch of artificial classical grandeur.)

Dr. Keil acquired title to the land in his name, and in the summer of 1844 he, his own family, and a few of his disciples made the riverboat trip just described and began to clear their land and prepare to receive the main body of his followers. They named the site, where they would build their town, "Bethel," a Biblical term for "The House of God" or "A Place of Worship." That winter of 1844-45 was a cold and difficult time for them. But by the spring of 1845, "Bethel" was ready to welcome the rest of the congregation. A steamboat brought them to Hannibal.

Living then in Hannibal was a youth who later became one of America's favorite sons and a famous
author—Mark Twain. In 1845 he was 10 years old and
still Sam Clemens. We know he loved the riverboat activity (that was one of the reasons he later became a
riverboat pilot) and it seems as likely as such things can
be that he ran down to the dock to watch Dr. Keil's
unusual company disembark. It's easy to visualize Sam
(in the role of Tom Sawyer) staring in fascination at the
immigrants, many still dressing like Swabian peasants
and probably singing German folk songs and hymns.

By the end of the summer of 1845, there were nearly
500 members at Bethel. Those joining the community all
signed a contract much like that signed in Father Rapp's
Harmony Society. And there were several other
similarities to the Harmony experience: scouts ahead to
find the land, a pioneering party to prepare the site for
the main body, the title to the land in the leader's name,
and, incidentally, the sale of whisky to the outside world.

Here is a summary of the principal provisions of the
Bethel contract:

1. Every member to put all he possesses into a common treasury.

2. This Society rests only on the Love of God, so that
   every opportunity for selfish gain shall be excluded.

3. If any brother should leave us, we cannot promise
   him a large requital, because the purpose of this
   Society is not to lay up treasures, and in this we
   base ourselves on the Word of God: "Having food
   and raiment, let us be content." But should a
   brother be no longer willing to remain with us, the
   Word of God also says, "You shall not let your
   brother go away from you empty." Thus, in this

matter, we shall find a way to deal with the brother, that we might abide in love.

4. Although we cannot promise much to anyone at the beginning, nevertheless the Society shall give to the single brother who leaves us twenty dollars for each year he was with the Society, as a compensation. And for families, forty dollars for each year. [Paragraphs 3 and 4 would apply to members who had brought in no money or property.]

5. If a brother who has brought in money or property leaves us, one-fourth of the value will be refunded each year for four years, without interest, so that at the end of four years it will all be returned to him. His house or land is left to the Society.

6. In case anyone should marry (after having joined the Society as a single person) and make a request for a house or land, this shall not be given to him until all other families who have already been with us are taken care of, after which he shall in his turn be taken care of.

7. This Society does not allow anyone to marry with such as do not believe in our teaching. This, however, does not mean that no one shall marry with a person of the outside world, because, if such a person is or will be a believer in the Word, he or she is welcomed by us.

8. Twelve men from among us must be elected who will look after the welfare of the Society in all things. These twelve men have the right, for the good of the Society, to draw up rules which are suitable to the circumstances, so that we may always abide in love and peace. [When Dr. Keil specified the number "twelve," it was probably not a

mere whim. Like Father Rapp, Dr. Keil based as
much as possible on passages in the Bible, where
the number "twelve" has, perhaps, some mystic sig-
nificance: the twelve tribes of Israel, the twelve
apostles.]

Though the Bethel contract resembled the Harmony
Society contract in several ways, there were also differen-
ces. Dr. Keil's statement had, overall, a more practical
tone. He was more open and less rigid than Father Rapp.
And, at Bethel, there was no mention of celibacy. Nor did
Dr. Keil set an example for that; he and Louisa already
had four children when they moved to Bethel and, while
they were there, they produced five more.

In addition to the members from Pennsylvania,
others, coming from Ohio, the Ohio River valley, and
Iowa, joined the Bethel Society. During the years 1846-48,
Bethel's population reached a temporary peak of about
1,000, but several hundred left after trying the life there
for a year or so. We don't know precisely why they
withdrew. Some may have been put off by Dr. Keil's
autocratic rule, by his emphasis on piety and worship, or
by the Society's indifference to worldly wealth. Most of his
original disciples, to whom he had preached in and
around Pittsburgh, stayed with him. They had come
knowing that he meant it when he said the purpose of the
Society would be worship and Christian love, not
luxurious living.

By the end of 1850, the population of the Bethel
community, including outlying farms, was about 650.
The U.S. census in the summer of 1850 counted 476
within the town itself. There, much building had
been done. In such work, they had had considerable
experience. For some of those carpenters and other
craftsmen, this was the FIFTH complete frontier
town they had built—Harmony, New Harmony,

Economy, Phillipsburg, and now Bethel! There were kilns, mills, shops, factories, and barns. Each family had its own house, many of them built of brick. And there were three large and especially impressive structures:

(1) A three-story edifice—some called it a mansion—for Dr. Keil. This was on a hilltop half a mile from Bethel itself. On its third floor was Dr. Keil's office. Here also was his laboratory—he continued to grow herbs and take care of the health of his followers, as a naturopathic physician. From his third-floor windows, he could observe activities in town and watch the cultivators working in the fields. By then, the Bethel property, most of it held in Dr. Keil's name, had increased to 4,000 acres. The building's second floor was one enormous open space, 36 x 60 feet, used as the community's banquet hall, dance floor, and meeting room. The ground floor comprised the living quarters of the good doctor and his wife and their nine children. In the basement was a wine cellar containing, according to a visitor of 1852, "30 barrels of wine." [4]

That visitor called Dr. Keil's house "kingly," and he thought its relative grandeur was inconsistent with the society's theme of "equality." Such critics did not take into account the background of the Bethelites. In the Europe from which these people came, it was considered fitting and right for the ruler—he was usually a king or prince—to live in a castle. Also, in this case, the building was partly a community facility.

Dr. Keil named his hilltop mansion "Elim," a place-name in the Old Testament. The Biblical Elim was an oasis of trees and water and a temporary camping spot for the Israelites on their exodus from Egypt *en route* to the Promised Land. Dr. Keil left us no explanation for his choice of the word Elim. Was he thinking of Bethel as a way-station *en route* to...to Oregon?...to Heaven? We do not know. In any case, the building is still standing and in excellent condition. The word "elim" means "large trees."

Dr. Keil's residence, known as "Elim," at Bethel, ca. 1852.

(2) A large multi-purpose building which the Bethelites called *"Das Grosse Haus"*—the big house. Here was the storeroom from which members withdrew whatever supplies and equipment they needed, and from which staples such as flour, meat, and cloth were distributed. Here also was a hotel, whose meals were said to have been sumptuous, and which was a money-maker for the society. The rest of "the big house" was a residence for all those who had no family with whom to live, and it included a dormitory for unmarried men.

(3) A magnificent church, admired by visitors and praised by residents of the surrounding area of Shelby County, who could hear its three bells ringing on Sunday mornings. The church, in all its details, was built by the community's own craftsmen. It was constructed of brick

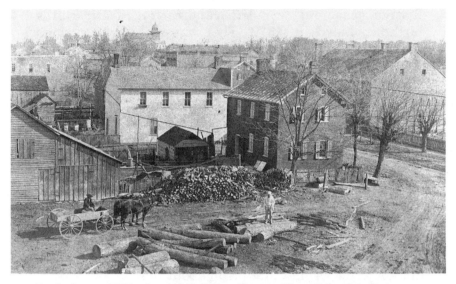

Bethel, ca. 1880. At right, *"Das Grosse Haus."* In the distance, the steeple of the church. In the foreground, tree trunks for the sawmill.

and stone, and the interior was finished in woodwork made from walnut trees. The floor was covered with red tiles. There was a gallery above the main floor for the Bethel band, a famous musical organization of 30 pieces, which played here on festive occasions. One of the annual

The Bethel band. ca. 1860.

festive occasions was the celebration of Dr. Keil's
birthday, March 6, 1812. This was also, by a curious
coincidence, the birthday of his wife—same day, month,
AND year!

Men and women sat on opposite sides of the church, a
practical arrangement which eliminated certain distractions which might have interfered with concentrating on
Dr. Keil's sermons. His sermons, delivered in German,
were not expositions of ecclesiastical dogma, because
there was none. He was completely independent of any
church denomination or creed. His sermons were com-
mentaries on Bible passages, with emphasis on moral
living and self-denial. There was no liturgy whatever, nor
were there ceremonies of baptism or confirmation. Marriages, however, there were—Dr. Keil, as we have noted,
did not agree with Father Rapp about that.

Were Dr. Keil's sermons eloquent and inspiring? Difficult to say, from this distance in time. Written opinions
by his contemporaries—the few such appraisals that
have survived—are contradictory in their evaluations,
which is not surprising since judging sermons is a highly
personal and subjective affair. He probably would not
have pleased a congregation of high-church Anglicans. It
appears that he was energetic and hortatory, sometimes
"stamping his feet and thumping his fists on the pulpit."
Perhaps the unfulfilled ambition of his youth, to be an
actor in the theater, gave his preaching style a dramatic
quality. The same critic who condemned Dr. Keil for
having such a large house and who was clearly anti-Keil
conceded that "Sometimes, it must be admitted, he really
preaches in an impressive manner..." [5] Coming grudging-
ly from a hostile source, this is high praise, indeed.

In the church, there was much singing and music.
Communion, or "the Lord's Supper," took the form of a big
Sunday dinner after the church service. With this was

their home-made wine—in the moderation consistent with self-denial and sober living, of course.

Of the hundreds who joined Dr. Keil at Bethel, only 61 brought any money to contribute. And the amounts were not large. They ranged from $2713 to $2. There were ten of $1000 or more. Seventeen were less than $100. Dr. Keil himself contributed $82. One former follower of Father Rapp, who had defected to Phillipsburg, contributed $630. The total fund at Bethel's beginning was about $31,000. (The real value of dollars at that time was, of course, much greater than it is today. In purchasing power, those 1845 dollar figures should be multiplied by about 15 to represent 1993 dollars.) The majority of Bethelites came bringing only willing hands. They were certainly not affluent, but neither were they especially interested in *becoming* affluent. Nevertheless, the members' energy and industry were such that, under the direction of Dr. Keil and the overseers and foremen he appointed, Bethel became productive and prosperous.

There were many industries and trades at Bethel. Most of the agricultural production was consumed intramurally, but some flour was sold. The Bethelites became specialists in four products which were much in demand: gloves, plows, wagons, and whisky.

> GLOVES. These were made of soft deerskin leather; the industry developed because of the large herds of wild deer in Missouri in those days. The men of Bethel shot the deer for meat, and the leather gloves were a by-product. Dr. Keil himself became a good horseman and marksman. The same querulous critic who censured Dr. Keil on other grounds also condemned him for spending so much time hunting. According to that 1852 visitor, Dr. Keil, when he first came to Bethel, didn't know how to ride a horse or load and fire a rifle, "but now he

Bethel's steam-powered mill for processing grain. Most buildings and houses at Bethel were made of brick, because suitable clay was available and because tall softwood trees for making construction lumber were not, though there were hardwood trees whose wood was excellent for furniture and woodwork. Aurora, by contrast, was in the midst of a fir forest, so all buildings there were made of wood.

excels all the colonists in these things because he does nothing else." [6] We know that Dr. Keil was busily occupied in many other activities, so the critic's petulance can be dismissed, but his observation does give a glimpse of life at Bethel and of Dr. Keil's character. The glove-makers submitted some of their handiwork to a fair in New York and won a prize.

PLOWS. The blacksmiths and carpenters produced the "Bethel Plow," which was highly regarded throughout the West. They could be sold as fast as they could be produced.

WAGONS. During the years 1845-1850, when Bethel's industries were developing, migration over the Oregon Trail was increasing, and some of the emigrants bought wagons made in Bethel. Those wagons were sturdy and, as word of their quality spread, the pioneers sought them for the rigorous journey over that rough trail.

WHISKY. Hundreds of barrels from the Bethel distillery were carted over the 45 miles of country road to Hannibal (population 2,020 in 1850). Bethel's brand name was "Golden Rule." Some was boated across the Mississippi River to the larger town of Quincy, Illinois.

Everywhere, Golden Rule whisky was highly esteemed. Unlike Father Rapp, Dr. Keil had not persuaded his followers to adopt a ban on whisky-drinking. In this respect, the Bethelites' sale of Golden Rule whisky was more straightforward than the sale of "Harmony" whisky by Father Rapp's distillers, who were selling something they would not drink themselves. But the Harmonists might well have replied, "If they don't drink ours, they will certainly drink someone else's; and, this way, at least we know they are drinking something clean, pure, and well made!" In allowing the drinking of whisky and the smoking of tobacco, Dr. Keil (he himself occasionally used snuff) was again less ascetic and perfectionist than ther Rapp.

ey accumulated from the sales of their products artly to add to the Society's real estate. In ght a 160-acre tract about 50 miles in Missouri's Adair County, and es- community there. It was on the

Main Street, Bethel, in 1870s.

Chariton River, and a water-powered mill was already in place. It was reportedly the largest mill west of the Mississippi River at that time. Ten houses were built and some families—about 25 people—moved there from Bethel. For the townsite, Dr. Keil designed a plat, with a central square and eight streets leading into it. He named it Nineveh, another Biblical place-name.

The original Nineveh, located on the Tigris River north of Babylon, was the capital of Assyria. It was completely destroyed by the Medes 612-606 B.C., and its ruins disappeared beneath the sands. In the years 1843-45, archeologists began to excavate those ruins. The digging continued during 1845-1850, with many finds of artistic and historic interest. Those discoveries were "in the news," and it is possible that word of them reached even unto Bethel, just when Dr. Keil was naming his new townsite. That this was the source of the name is mere conjecture, of course; it is at least a timely coincidence.

By 1852, more houses and shops had been built, 150 people were living at Nineveh, and the land holding had been expanded to 2,000 acres. The Ninevites converted the water-powered mill to steam power, and sold milled products—flour, lumber, etc. They also made and sold woven textiles (the looms were powered by the steam mill), leather, and shoes. And they operated a ferry across the river just below the mill. Dr. Keil had a house at Nineveh, which he used on his occasional visits. The site of Nineveh is now the town of Connelsville.

How shall we, in retrospect, appraise Dr. Keil and his Bethel-Nineveh Society? Clearly, that can only be done in the context of their own values and objectives. They lived simply, aiming to get through this earthly life peacefully, in Christian love and the hope of heaven. They were, and wanted to be, isolated from the national political and cultural milieu surrounding them. Bethel was called "The Christian Community."

Bethel school house, in 1870s. At rear, the Bethel church. Note the church steeple's platform, from which the band played.

Such visitors as came to Bethel were usually curiosity-seekers or critics who judged what they saw by the values of "the world." Applying such values, they naturally saw much to call quaintness, foolishness, or failure. But the fact that the core of Dr. Keil's followers—600 or more—remained loyal implies a substantial degree of success. And their productive and adequately prosperous lives should have betokened stability and contentment. Even so, there began to appear, in the early 1850's, a certain restlessness in the community and in Dr. Keil himself...a restless spirit which seemed to be saying, "Move on, onward, westward...to Oregon!"

Chapter 6
From Bethel to Aurora

Dr. Keil's decision to "go west" was the resultant of several forces acting upon him: the supposed attractions of Oregon, his own restless disposition, and discontent or apprehension about Bethel's location.

The eyes and thoughts of Dr. Keil and his followers were turned toward the West by the streams of pioneers passing through Missouri, the great wagon trains assembling at St. Joseph or Independence, and the fact that some of those adventurers were traveling in wagons they had bought at Bethel. The reports coming back from Oregon, some of them gross exaggerations, added a little fantasy to the enticement—a moderate and salubrious climate, rich soil, tranquility. Moreover, the land out there was FREE! The Oregon Donation Land Act, which Congress passed in September 1850, granted an entire section (640 acres) to any family settling there by December 1855. The Act applied to the "Oregon Country," which included what is now the State of Washington.

Those seeds of temptation fell upon fertile ground in Dr. Keil's imagination. Years before, in New York City, he was already seen as "restless" and "a dreamer." He was temperamentally suited to adventure. His followers, too, were prone to travel, many having dared the risky business of crossing the Atlantic in small sailing ships. Their

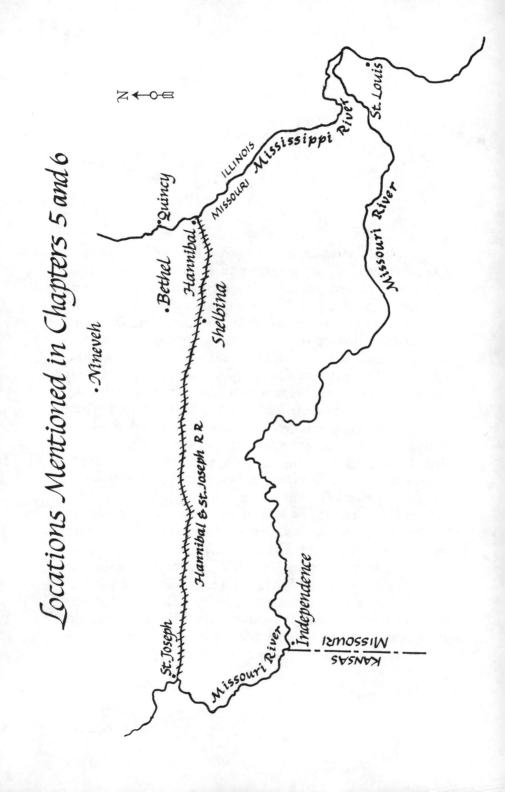

Locations Mentioned in Chapters 5 and 6

further peregrinations with Father Rapp showed their willingness, perhaps even eagerness, to move on.

At the same time, conditions in Missouri were becoming less congenial. One cause of uneasiness was the slavery problem. Missouri had been admitted to the Union in 1821 as a "slave" state; that is, its constitution permitted slavery. There were slaves in Missouri, especially in the southeast portion where cotton was grown. But there was anti-slavery sentiment in the state, too, and there were vociferous confrontations between the anti- and pro-slavery factions. In this sense, Missouri was a microcosm of the entire nation, which was suffering severe sectional strains. The "Missouri Compromise," whereby Missouri had been admitted as a "slave" state and Maine as a "free" state (thus maintaining the equilibrium by adding two Senators to each faction) was one of many maneuvers devised by moderate representatives from the North and South to keep the Union together. But now, after 30 years, compromises were becoming ever more difficult. It seemed all too likely that the aggressive threats by the hard-liners on both sides would eventually lead to a violent conflict, which one could escape by moving to Oregon.

Another development (ominous from the viewpoint of separatist utopians) was the growth of population and industry in Missouri. This "progress" was what Dr. Keil and the Bethelites had sought to leave behind them when they moved away from Pittsburgh. Now, even here, "the world" was crowding in on them. An example was the construction in 1852 of the "Hannibal & St. Joseph R.R.," which crossed the state south of Bethel. Indeed, the railroad builders had planned to put the line through Bethel itself! The industrious Bethelites might produce exports to be shipped out on the freight cars. And Bethel was then the largest town in Shelby County. (The county seat, Shelbyville, had 359 inhabitants in 1850.) But Dr. Keil

objected. That must have dumbfounded the railroad offi-
cials, who were being importuned and bribed by most
townsite proprietors to bring the line *to* their villages.
Because of Dr. Keil's startling opposition, the railroad did
not profane Bethel's privacy. But a "station stop" was
established at a small village called Shelbina, 13 miles
south of Bethel. This was much closer than Hannibal. Dr.
Keil's disciples might go there, though it still meant three
or four uncomfortable hours on the wooden bench of a
jolting wagon. And who knew what temptations or cor-
rupting influences might seduce the simple Bethelite once
amidst the handful of homespun inhabitants at Shelbina,
with its railroad trains. It was a sinister portent.

These incursions of "the world" into the Bethel utopia,
and the falling away of some of the members from strict
piety, were emphasized by Dr. Keil as a reason for leaving
Bethel. He wrote later (in a letter dated October 13, 1855)
that he had problems at Bethel because the people were
not submitting to discipline nor giving "heed to the day of
the Lord," but were letting their children grow up "in a
blasphemous and unspiritual life." [7]

The impact of all these forces—some pulling, some
pushing—was irresistible. In the spring of 1853, Dr. Keil
sent a group of nine scouts to find a new site out in the
Oregon Country. The party included Adam Schuele, one
of the trio who in 1843 had chosen the location for Bethel.
The other eight were Christian Giesy, his wife Emma (*nee*
Wagner), John Ginger, Joseph and Adam Knight
(brothers), Michael Schaeffer, and John and Stans Stauffer
(brothers). Christian Giesy, then 49 years old, was the
party's leader. He was from the large Giesy family who were
among Dr. Keil's earliest converts. His wife's family had
come from Germany to Harmony in 1805, withdrew to
Phillipsburg in 1832, and there became followers of Dr. Keil.

In that spring of 1853, there were many wagon trains,
large and small, heading westward over the Oregon Trail,

and the scouting party joined one of them. After not more than the usual adventures and difficulties, they reached The Dalles late that summer. By 1853, there were riverboats on the Columbia and Willamette rivers. The nine scouts went down the Columbia River to Fort Vancouver. It is not reported that they visited Portland, but surely they must have done so, because it was by then the largest and most developed townsite in the Territory, with a population of about 1,500 and a connection by steamship with San Francisco. In the years 1852–53, the steamships sometimes came directly to Portland; at other times, they stopped at Astoria, from which a steamboat brought the passengers and mail up to Portland. By 1854, the steamships came regularly to Portland.

By the fall of 1853, earlier pioneers had already claimed much of the desirable land in and around Portland and in the Willamette and Tualatin valleys, but, at Fort Vancouver, the scouts heard of what was described as attractive land in southwestern Washington Territory. They went there and established claims near the mouth of the Willapa River, not far from the present town of Raymond. Their claims were close to Willapa Bay, famous for its oysters even in those days.

The nine pioneers set to work building cabins and clearing small open spaces in the dense primeval forest. In the spring of 1854, after an uncomfortable winter, Joseph and Adam Knight returned to Bethel to report what they had seen and done, leaving the other seven scouts to prepare for the arrival of Dr. Keil and his followers.

The Knights' enthusiasm, though it turned out to be based on misjudgment and illusion, convinced Dr. Keil. Preparations were begun to move part of the Bethel community to the west coast. The rest of the Bethelites, or as many as wished, would come sometime later, after building had progressed.

Dr. Keil in 1855 when he was 43 years old.

By the spring of 1855, the covered wagons were ready
and Dr. Keil had selected those he wanted to be in this
first party.

One small group, eager to begin the adventure and
reach Oregon before the fall rains if possible, left on April
1st. That early train, consisting of six wagons pulled by
mules, was led by Peter Klein. A few weeks later, the
main body of emigrants was ready. But shortly before
the scheduled departure, Dr. Keil's oldest child, Willie,
became ill with malaria, which in those days was
widespread in the damp areas of the Mississippi valley.
Willie, now 18 years old, did not want to be left behind—
Dr. Keil, his wife, and their other eight children would all
be going. He beseeched his father not to leave him at
Bethel, and Dr. Keil promised—and apparently it was a
very solemn promise—to take him along. A wagon was
converted to an ambulance, in which Willie was to travel
on a cot. Dr. Keil delayed the departure for a few days,

expecting Willie to recover and be able to drive one of the wagons, which he had been looking forward to doing. But, despite Dr. Keil's medicinal ministrations, Willie died, May 19, 1855. Dr. Keil decided to take Willie's body with them, to be buried in the Oregon Country.

This episode has been the subject of many articles and stories, some of them making it rather eccentric or even grotesque. It has also been suggested that it was Dr. Keil's way of teaching his disciples that promises must be kept, although he must have felt sure, according to his own Christian theology, that the real Willie was no longer in Missouri but in heaven. Perhaps the decision is understandable simply as a father's wish to have his son's body buried at the new homesite. In any case, it was not difficult to convert the ambulance into a hearse. Willie's body was place in a tin-lined coffin, which was filled with alcohol from the Bethel distillery. When the wagons headed westward, on May 23, 1855, Willie's coffin wagon was in the lead, where it remained during the five-month long odyssey.

At Willie's death, Dr. Keil composed a hymn, which the departing colonists sang, and which they sang again when Willie's body was buried at Willapa. The hymn was also used occasionally for later funerals at Aurora. This is the first verse, in the original German:

> Das Grab ist tief und stille
> Und schauderhaft sein Rand;
> Es deckt mit tiefer Hülle
> Ein unbekanntes Land.

Here is a free translation (without any attempt at rhyming) of that verse and a few other lines which together give some idea of Dr. Keil's style and mystical spirit.

Deep is the grave, and silent;
Terrifying is its brink.
It covers, like a dark veil,
An unknown realm.
Only through this dark doorway
Can we regain our home.
The poor heart here on earth
Is tossed by many a storm.
True peace it finds only
When it beats no more.

Leaving Andrew Giesy, Jr. (then 37 years old and a younger brother of Christian Giesy) in charge at Bethel, Dr. Keil and his wagon train, on their first day of travel, reached Nineveh. There, several more families and wagons joined them. Then they all turned toward St. Joseph and the beginning of the Oregon Trail. It was a long train of 35 wagons, some pulled by mules but most of them pulled by oxen, which could subsist better on the prairie grass.

In a letter written June 24, 1855 "on the bank of the Platte River" near Fort Kearney, Dr. Keil described the trek across Missouri and into the plains:[7]

After our departure from Nineveh, our journey to St. Joseph went very well. The intermittent rain we had was good for our cattle. Our greatest difficulty was that our livestock would stray away and it was a tedious search to recover it. The roads are bad. [After they had crossed the Missouri River at St. Joseph]...quite a different spirit made itself felt. All the anxiety and fear that was in the human heart turned to me for comfort. Strangers, respectable men, warned me and pleaded with me not to cross the plains with my people in such a cruel time

because they said the reports were so bad
that it would cost the life of every person.
They said eight thousand Indians had col-
lected between Kearney and Laramie, had
robbed the immigrants of their clothing, livestock and everything else, and sent the
people back; and that the Indians had occupied Fort Laramie and killed all the soldiers. I stood still a few moments and did not
know what I should say to all that. Then the
spirit came over me and asked me if I intended to end my days in a different manner
than I had managed everything through all
my days [meaning, presumably, with self-con-
fidence and faith in God's providence]. So I
went away from the camp and ascended to
the top of a high hill to pray. I rested a while,
then the spirit spoke thus: If what you have
done during your life to this hour is not
enough to defeat all your enemies, then no
other sacrifice will be found for you. I vowed
three times to cast down the first enemy force
that confronted my people, though they
might gather by thousands. When I came
back to the camp, all fear had vanished from
me and from those who belonged to me. My
wish was that a thousand or more enemies
might assemble at once, for I felt that
thousands and more would have to fall in an
instant at a glance from me.

When we started our journey across the
plains, we found by the trail a little wagon
such as children play with, loaded with
provisions. We did not know to whom it
belonged. The next day on our journey we
found the wagon again, but there was no one

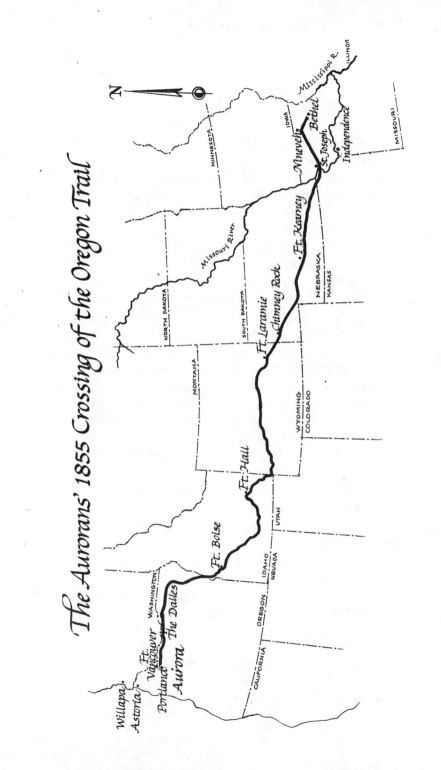

The Aurorans' 1855 Crossing of the Oregon Trail

near it. I left two horsemen behind with orders that they should search the surrounding
region for the man to find if he might be
sleeping in the grass nearby. I went ahead
with the wagons, and said that if I should
find him, I would send them word. When we
had traveled for miles, the man himself came
directly across the prairie. He was a German
locksmith who had been in America for only a
half-year; he was straying about the prairie
like a sheep. I asked him where he intended
to go. He answered that he did not know.
When I wanted to ask him some more questions, he fell into a faint. I took him up, as a
father would his son. He is a good boy and
helps drive the cattle.

There are a few hundred wagons behind
us, which we have passed. We are always one
or two days journeys ahead of them. Fear is
unknown to us. Indeed, we have not as yet
seen one Indian. Before we reached the Platte
River we saw thousands and thousands of
buffaloes. I galloped into the midst of them,
wounded one, and all the dogs chased after it.

Yesterday evening we came to the Platte
River. At our campground is a grave. Beside it
William's wagon is standing. William goes
ahead of us. Everyone has noticed this wagon
especially, but no one has ever asked what we
convey in it. He [William's body] is still in
exactly the same condition as he was when
we left Bethel. We have not had to add any
more alcohol.

Our wagons are all just as good as they
were at the beginning of our journey. The
stock is actually in better condition. Ruge

[Karl Ruge] broke an axle, but Link [George Link] made one which is better than the old one was. We still have everything. We have not lost even a dog. The dogs allow no one to come on to the campground. When I blow the trumpet [his signal to start moving] there is a tumult like an earthquake. Willie goes ahead and we follow him. Cordial greetings to all of you.

Farewell till we meet again.

When the plodding caravaneers reached Fort Laramie, Wyoming, they found it intact and the soldiers alive. The rumor of their massacre had been a great exaggeration, as rumors tend to be—passed on, as they are, from one emotional person to another, each trying to make the story more sensational. From Fort Laramie, Dr. Keil was able to send back to Bethel a reassuring letter which contained these observations:[7]

I find all things different on the plains than had been reported to me. [He had been told they would not find wood for campfires.] In general, there is more wood on the plains than the people in Europe have.

The passage through the Platte and Laramie rivers is nothing. It is astonishing that men at times make a fuss about something which finally turns out to be nothing; Any dog can run through these rivers.

From Kearney to Laramie we had currant and gooseberry pies that were better than we had in Missouri. I have lived in the same manner as I used to at home. As far along as this side of the Platte River, we had our spinach every day.

At the so-called Courthouse Rock and Chimney Rock, the mountains reminded me of the shape of the fortress at Erfurt. [Erfurt was the city in Germany near which he lived as a youth.]

[Even though bands of reportedly belligerent Indians had gathered around Fort Laramie and to the west, Dr. Keil decided to push on.] Tomorrow we will start and proceed toward hell. Do not dispose of your homes until you receive further information from me. [The plan had been for the rest of the Bethelites to sell their property and join the new colony on the west coast when it had been established.]

Dr. Keil's next letter, from Oregon, reported the successful conclusion of the journey. [7]

In my last report, from Laramie, I stated that from there we would move toward hell. My prophecy came true. The uprising among the Sioux Indians around Laramie was enormous so that no one dared to leave the fort. But we were made without fear. We met hundreds of Indians who were glad when they saw my face. I have had all power over the Indians and could do with them as I desired. [This is a reference to the often-mentioned magnetic power of his countenance.] Many a time I have been surrounded by fifty to sixty Indians. I gave them tobacco which pleased them greatly. Our little children would run ahead of the wagon train into the midst of the Indians. They gave the Indian children bread and all sorts of other things, which pleased the older Indians very much.

> We came to places where there were so many
> Indians we could not count them. In short,
> my happinesses on the plains were the meet-
> ings with the Indians. With great difficulty
> [because of the trail] we reached the Umatilla
> Valley, lost some cattle, and camped among
> those Indians, who brought us potatoes, peas,
> and onions, and who again were very friendly
> toward us.

Among Aurora Colony descendants, there is an oral
tradition that one of the reasons the Indians treated Dr.
Keil's caravan with friendly respect was Willie's casket at
the head of the train. And that idea has been featured in
articles about Aurora. Certainly, the Indians were much
interested in "spirits" and medicine men, and a corpse
pickled in whisky at the head of the procession might
have been, for them, "Big Medicine," indeed. Dr. Keil
himself never mentioned that possibility. He said, as we
have just read, that no one asked what was in the leading
wagon, though it was not at all a secret. Perhaps the
Indians learned about the coffin from some of the members of the wagon train, and, if they did, it might well
have induced them to approach the train with awe rather
than hostility.

At The Dalles, Dr. Keil and his caravan were met by
Christian Giesy, who led them to the Willapa site where
the scouts had established claims. They reached Willapa
November 1, 1855.

After Dr. Keil's report of the triumphantly successful
crossing of the plains, his letters from Willapa were a very
discouraging contrast. He did not like the location. What
he may have said to the scouts who chose it has not been
recorded, but here is what he wrote to Bethel: [7]

> The land itself cannot be surpassed in the
> whole creation with regard to fertility, for

everything that is planted grows here in abundance. But no one knows what he is to do with the crops. [There were very few people thereabouts and no market for products; most settlement was in the Willamette Valley.]

It would be impossible for us to raise the material for our clothing. There are no sheep here. There would be no feed for them. We could not use carding machines and looms here, unless the wool were obtained from California or from South America. Neither could there be tanneries; the hides would have to be imported from afar, perhaps even from the States. However, a distillery could dispose of its products to the few oyster fishers who live by the bay.

If I wanted to build houses of the type we had in Missouri for those who are here at this time in this valley, the initial cost would be no less than a hundred thousand dollars. There is not enough open land and it is too difficult to clear the giant trees of this virgin forest.

If you have not already sold there, then I advise you not to sell an acre of land that you own, for I believe that such houses as you have there cannot be found either in Oregon or the Washington Territory.

The colonists buried Willie's body and spent a miserable winter in the damp dense forest around Willapa. Early in the spring, Dr. Keil and many of his followers came up to Portland, where they arrived about the first of March 1856. Those who had already established claims at Willapa, including Christian Giesy, remained there, along with some of the new arrivals.

In addition to the 150 pioneers who came in Dr. Keil's train[8] and those in the small preceding train of Peter Klein, several (perhaps seven) had come by steamship via the Isthmus of Panama route and a dozen had come by ship around Cape Horn. Those numbers are approximations—they are deduced from the recollections of elderly Aurorans many years later. Dr. Keil and company were not strong on record-keeping; the days of statisticians, data banks, and archivists had not yet arrived. But, on the basis of available estimates, there were now about 175 ex-Bethelites in "the Oregon Country," dispersed at and around Willapa and Portland, all in varying degrees of discomfort. That spring, Dr. Keil began searching for a suitable site for the new colony.

He found a desirable tract on the Pudding River between Oregon City and Salem, which was for sale. It comprised a quarter-section owned by David Smith and an adjoining quarter-section owned by George White. Dr. Keil bought the 320 acres, and the colonists gradually moved there and began construction of the new utopia.

Chapter 7

Colony Days at Aurora

The site that became Aurora was on a small stream called Deer Creek, near its junction with Pudding River. The previous owners, who settled on their claims in 1847-48, had constructed a dam on the creek. This provided a millrace, and they had built a sawmill and a mill for grinding grain. The mills came with the property. Dr. Keil named the site "Aurora," in honor of one of his daughters. For many years, it was known as "Aurora Mills."

Also on the property was a log cabin. Dr. Keil selected about a dozen men from among his flock then in Portland and sent them to live in that cabin and construct the Colony's first building. With them he sent one woman, probably the wife of one of the men; her job was to keep plenty of good food on the table. They went there in May 1856, and the construction crew began cutting the huge fir trees, sawing them into lumber, and building "*Das Grosse Haus.*" This "Big House" would be a temporary residence for Dr. Keil and his family, and for the single men. It would also contain the Colony storehouse and a meeting room. Gradually, individual houses would be built for each Colony family.

During 1856, the number in the construction brigade increased to 20 or more. Dr. Keil laid down a rule: Every morning, before breakfast, each four-man team must cut down one tree. But if there was a shortage of meat, then

Aurora's *"Grosse Haus,"* built 1856–57, was a temporary residence for the Keil family, a dormitory for bachelors, and the Colony storehouse, until larger buildings were constructed.

(instead of cutting a tree) they must shoot one deer— before breakfast! (The woods in the Willamette Valley were full of deer in those days.)

The 27 years of Aurora's existence as a communal society fall conveniently into four periods:

1. May 1856 to October 3, 1863, the date when a great wagon train brought 252 more members from Bethel to Aurora.

2. October 1863 to October 4, 1870, when the first railroad train arrived at Aurora.

3. October 1870 to Dr. Keil's death, December 30, 1877.

4. The disintegration, December 1877 to 1883. This period and the final dissolution and distribution of property are discussed in Chapter 8.

1856–1863

This was the pioneering era—rustic, simple, Arcadian. Dr. Keil demonstrated his power of leadership by holding the members together, maintaining a sense of Colony unity while they were scattered in Willapa, Portland, and Aurora. For about a year, Dr. Keil lived mostly in Portland, with his wife and eight children. But he made many trips to Aurora, staying there some of the time, to help with and plan the work. His trip would have been by riverboat between Portland and Oregon City, and by coach or wagon between Oregon City and Aurora. He could have made the trip, one way, in about half a day.

It is sometimes asserted that Dr. Keil chose the Aurora site because it was isolated. But by 1856 most land in the Willamette Valley had been claimed, either under the Donation Land Act or the Homestead Act, so that farmers and villages were not far away, and development was increasing. Also, Aurora was on the main road between Oregon City and Salem. Dr. Keil did want isolation from "the world," in the sense of its worldliness and unspirituality, but he was practical enough to see the advantages, indeed the necessity, of doing business and trading with people outside the Colony.

Dr. Keil was a prudent planner. When the Colonists had cut and sawed the trees on the Aurora site (lumber was very expensive to buy, but they got theirs free), they planted extensive orchards. Before those trees became productive, Dr. Keil bought fruit from neighboring farmers—apples at $1 a bushel, for example. Then he asked his people to save their apple peelings and use them to make cider vinegar, which he sold back to the neighbors for $1.50 a gallon. By such close husbandry, he built up his treasury; and when less efficient farmers got into debt and had to sell their land, Dr. Keil bought it. He and the Aurorans eventually owned more than 15,000 fertile acres, scattered over three counties.

While Dr. Keil was living, intermittently, in Portland, he practiced as a naturopathic physician. He was well known in the region. He was mentioned in a reminiscence by Sydney Moss, who was living in Oregon City then. Mr. Moss had arrived there in 1842, and operated the first and, for some years, the only hotel in Oregon City. He knew Dr. Keil and wrote this about him and Aurora:

> Dr. Keil was the agent [of the Aurora Colony]. They bought the land in common. The title was made to Dr. Keil, and each one in the colony had an interest in the purchase. He was a European and a very clever man.[9]

By 1857, *Das Grosse Haus* was sufficiently complete for the Keils to move there from Portland. Others came with them. Farm houses were built by the communal carpenters. Some Colony families bought land on their own, within a few miles of Aurora, but remained part of the Aurora community. Because of its dispersed beginnings, widely scattered farms, and the private ownership of some properties, Aurora was never quite as "communal" as Bethel.

But the Aurorans were held together by several other forces besides their idea of communal Christian living. One was music. They had had an excellent band at Bethel. The music master there, Henry Conrad Finck, did not come out in the 1855 wagon train, but several musicians did. A "colony" band was active early in 1856, while the members were marking time in Portland. They would work at their various trades and crafts during the day and practice music in the evenings. This item appeared in the *Oregonian* March 22, 1856:

We were favored a few evenings since by a serenade from the "Germania Band" of this city. We have seldom heard better music than this band discourses. We understand that this company of musicians number 10 persons, all Germans and relatives who crossed the Plains last year.

Aurora Colonist George Wolfer playing an ophicleide (from Greek "ophis," serpent), so named because it is the older wooden instrument called a "serpent," but with finger keys added.

By the following year, they had moved to Aurora. Now known as the "Aurora Colony Band," they played at a Fourth of July celebration at Butteville (a village near Champoeg) in 1857. In 1858, they were hired to play for the "Old Settlers' Ball" in Oregon City.

Dr. Keil, though not a member of the band (he did play the harmonica!) actively supported it, and singing and music in general. In addition to the funeral piece "Deep is the Grave" mentioned in Chapter 6, he composed other hymns (not only the words but the music) and also marches. The Aurora Colony archives contain a piece, *"Schützen Marsch"* (Sharpshooters March), with the notation "Composed by Dr. Wm. Keil, arranged by F. Giesy." Another march is inscribed "Composed by Dr. Keil."

Besides music, another factor holding the Colony members together was the school. This was taught by Karl Ruge, who was in Dr. Keil's 1855 wagon train. "Professor" Ruge was a university graduate who left Germany about 1849. The school was conducted at first in both German and English, but later entirely in English.

The Aurora Band. Seated, second from left with the snare drum, is Dr. Keil's son Emanuel.

Also a uniting force was Dr. Keil's preaching. During this period, the church had not yet been built, but he could hold meetings in The Big House, and he could also counsel and exhort. He taught persevering industry (though he laid this on less heavily than Father Rapp had done), humility, simplicity, prayer, self-sacrifice, and neighborly love. Perhaps it was in this spirit that, in 1862, he allowed a Colony member to help a neighbor, outside the Colony, who was stricken with smallpox. That was a virulent and often fatal disease in those days. The Colony member, John Wolfer, asked Dr. Keil if he should go to the neighbor's assistance and Dr. Keil agreed. Unfortunately, the good samaritan brought the disease back into the Colony, and several Colony members, including John's wife, died of it. Among the others who died were four of Dr. Keil's children. His son Elias died November 22, 1862, aged 19; Louisa, December 11, aged 18; Glorianda, December 11, aged 15; and Aurora, December 14, aged 13.

Dr. Keil's response to this tragedy, according to some old members' reminiscences, was to withdraw into himself, speaking to no one for days at a time. Such an initial reaction was, perhaps, understandable, but it continued for some time, with the result that development at Aurora suffered. When the big wagon train's 252 new members arrived ten months later, some of them were distressed at Dr. Keil's lack of the strong, assertive, and enthusiastic leadership they remembered when he was at Bethel. Eventually he came to see the deaths of his children as God's will; he recovered and went on to lead the Colony during its period of greatest growth and success. But a few members remained disenchanted, which may have contributed to Aurora's later changes away from communalism.

Dr. Keil's Job-like acceptance of the children's deaths was recorded by author Charles Nordhoff who visited Aurora in 1873. Dr. Keil took him on a tour, and they came upon the childrens' graves.

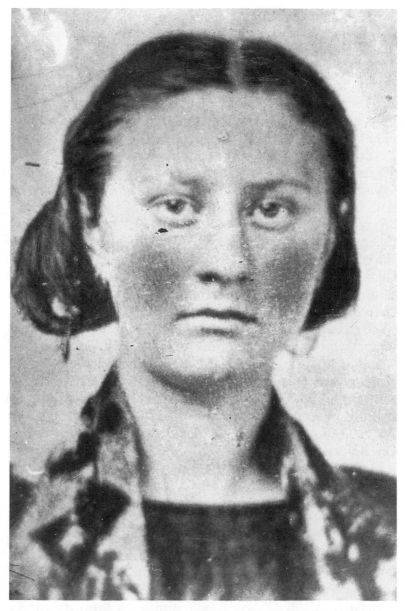

Aurora Keil (1849–1862), probably taken in 1862 when she
was 13 years old, and not long before her death.

"He said, 'Here lie my children.... One after the other I laid them here. It was hard to bear; but now I can thank God for that, too.' Then, after a minute's silence, he turned upon me with sombre eyes and said, 'To bear all that comes upon us in silence, in quiet, without noise, or outcry, or excitement, or useless repining—that is to be a man, and that we can do only with God's help.'"[10]

William Keil in the 1870s.
He died December 30, 1877 at the age of 65.

Of Dr. Keil's four remaining children, August had
been sent back to Bethel about 1862 as his father's
viceroy, to assist Andrew Giesy, Jr. in administering that
community. There, in 1864, August married Rosina
Forstner. He was then 26 years old and she was 24. (For
her family history, see Chapter 9.) August was not very
efficient as his father's vicar, according to some accounts.
He died at Bethel in 1901, at the age of 63.

Aurora, at the time of the arrival of the large wagon
train October 3, 1863, consisted of the communal building
("The Big House") and, a little distance away, the two
mills. A few houses were hidden among the fir trees, with
others scattered on outlying farms. When the 252 new
members arrived after their six-month journey, they did
not recognize the Aurora site as even a village. That is
shown in the following excerpts from the diary of George
Wolfer. He recorded that, at the Cascades, the wagons
had been ferried across the Columbia River on a flat boat.

> From there "we proceeded down the north
> bank of the Columbia with our slow-moving
> oxen.... We again ferried the Columbia a little
> above Vancouver [back to the Oregon side]
> and laid over for a day. Here we bought a big
> fat beef. We saw a little bit of Portland as we
> continued on our way next day; we followed
> the east bank of the Willamette River south.
> A little south of Oregon City our last stop was
> made.... All of us were expectant the next
> day.... Toward noon we arrived at the old
> bridge over the Pudding River. Crossing over
> the bridge, we began the long winding climb
> over a narrow timber road to Ziegler's barn.
> Here I met Henry Fry, whom I know well
> [from earlier days at Bethel] and I asked him,
> 'How far is it to Aurora?' He replied, 'You are

right *in* Aurora.' This so took the wind out of my sails that I was speechless.... We had given little thought as to what Aurora looked like and were rather loathe to accept the truth, so disturbing was the effect. [Perhaps they had anticipated a town like Bethel, with its large brick buildings and neatly laid out streets.] After spending several days in Aurora, where there was considerable feasting and merrymaking over our safe arrival, we [the Wolfers] and several other families were sent [by Dr. Keil] out on the great prairie lands east of Aurora that had very recently been acquired by Doc [the members' rather familiar nickname for Dr. Keil] for $3,000 cash." [11]

The 1863 wagon train was led by "Captain" Christopher Wolff. He was a university graduate who had left Germany about 1849. At Bethel he had been one of Dr. Keil's close associates. All of the doctor's letters sent back to Bethel were addressed to Christopher Wolff, who read them aloud on Sundays to the congregation in church. At Aurora, "Captain" Wolff became "Professor" Wolff, as he joined "Professor" Ruge in teaching in the Colony school.

1863–1870

This was Aurora's "Golden Age." During this period, its principal buildings were constructed—the church, the hotel, and Dr. Keil's 3-story residence. The Keil house was sufficiently completed by 1865 for the doctor, his wife, and their three children remaining at Aurora (Emanuel, Frederick, and Amelia) to move in. It included an apothecary's shop, where the doctor prepared his medicines and remedies. This house is still standing, though privately owned, and has been restored to Colony-days appearance.

The hotel included a dining room that became famous throughout the state. Even before this, *Das Grosse Haus* had been a popular meal-stop for stagecoaches. With the completion of the hotel, this feature became a principal money-maker for the Colony. An overnight or weekend stay at the hotel, with the lavish meals, was a gala outing for Oregonians. The menu featured, among other things, ham, sausage, and venison.

Buggy and pair, in front of the Aurora Colony Hotel.

For a special banquet or occasion at the hotel, the Aurora Colony Band would play. Sometimes the band assembled to greet an incoming train. Or it might play from the band platform atop the hotel. The 1863 covered wagon caravan had brought several more musicians, and the band had grown to 35 pieces. Also, there was now a second band, for younger men and boys, called the "Pie and Beer" band. The professional quality of the music was enhanced late in 1862 by the arrival of Bethel's Music Man—Henry C. Finck. He had first come to Bethel in 1849, selling musical instruments. He married a daughter of a Bethel family and became an informal member of the communal society, building up the Bethel band and giving music lessons. His wife died in 1858, but not before bearing him five children. In the fall of 1862, Professor Finck brought the young children to Aurora, traveling first to New York, then by steamship to Panama, railroad across the isthmus, and steamship to Portland. This route—possibly safer and certainly more comfortable than six months in a covered wagon—took them five weeks.

One of the Music Man's sons—Henry Theophilus Finck, educated in Aurora's school by Professors Ruge and Wolff—was Oregon's first student to enter Harvard University, where he enrolled in 1872. From 1881 to 1924, he was the music critic for the *New York Evening Post*. In 1873, his father moved from Aurora to Portland, and later to California.

The Colony church was completed and dedicated in 1867. Its steeple was 114 feet high. Around the steeple were two platforms or balconies where the Colony band could play, sending music floating through the air above the Aurorans. That church was demolished in 1912, and the hotel in 1934.

There was also a "Park House." This was on a hilltop west of the town, amidst several acres of park-like trails. There were benches and a rose garden. Here were held picnics, dances, band concerts, and the numerous fetes which were an important part of Colony life. On these occasions, the area was sometimes lit by colored lanterns. Dr. Keil, describing the setting, said, "On May Day, after dark, the scene could be from the Arabian Nights. To that glitter add the sound of music and the lilt of song and the young people happily dancing, and what a joyous spectacle..."[12]

The Aurora Colony Church (1867–1912). Note the two platforms or balconies, from which the Colony band sometimes played.

It was a simple and unpretentious life. The women dressed in homemade clothes of calico, even when going to church. At weddings, there was much laughing and joking. The men were described as "good-natured" but not remarkably ambitious. Everyone had what little he required without working very hard. The pace of work was steady but not pressed. And there was flexibility and variety as to the type of work; if there was a need for carpenters, the shoemaker and tailor, if they were not busy, would become carpenters. In summer, all hands turned towards the fields and crops. Aurora had the best orchards in Oregon and an excellent system of agriculture.

Interior of the Aurora Colony Church. Note the wood stove with a steel drum for greater radiation of heat.

During the period 1863-70, some of those who had remained at Willapa rejoined Dr. Keil and their old friends at Aurora, now that the town was beginning to flourish. One was John Stauffer. He was one of the nine scouts who came to Willapa in 1853, and he had remained on his claim there. He moved to Aurora in 1865 and built a large Colony-style log house on a farm just south of Aurora. That house is now a museum owned by the Aurora Colony Historical Society.

More wagon trains arrived during these years. In 1865, "Captain" John Vogt led eleven wagons, all pulled by mules. He brought about 60 people. In 1867, "Captain" George Link brought 75 people, in 15 wagons, all pulled by oxen. By the end of 1867, Aurora had a population of about 600.

Among these Aurorans were now three men whose backgrounds were rather different from the pietistic Swabians, Bavarians, and German-Swiss who comprised most of the Colonists. These three were Christopher Wolff, Karl Ruge, and Henry C. Finck, the musician. These men had not come to America as followers of a "separatist" like George Rapp. Herr Wolff was a graduate of Göttingen University, and "Professor" Ruge had studied to be a teacher. These two left Germany after the failure of the 1848-49 attempt by "liberals" to impose constitutional monarchy on the German rulers. A group of such men, largely from the professional middle class (teachers, lawyers, administrators, etc.) had met in the spring of 1849 at Frankfurt, drafted a constitution providing for a limited monarchy, and offered the crown, on those terms, to King Frederick of Prussia. He turned these "radicals" down—their constitution was too liberal, and also the idea of their offering him a crown implied that it was theirs to offer, rather than his as a divine right. The delegates went home in disarray, accelerated by the Prussian army, which was dominated by the landed aristocracy (the Junkers). We don't know what role Wolff and Ruge may have had in the movement, but they sympathized with it. When it failed, they and many others emigrated.

The ability of Dr. Keil to accept and work with these "intellectuals" shows that he was not as narrow or provincial as some writers or critics have implied. And their being comfortable in his Christian commune suggests at least a tolerance for his preaching. There appears to have been no theological gulf between Dr. Keil and these teachers. We might conclude that the common denominator that enabled these men to work together was their general belief in Jesus' teachings. We do know that Professor Wolff was a devout Lutheran. Perhaps this

"Professor" Karl Ruge,
teacher at the Aurora Colony school.

unity among diverse men was facilitated because, at
Bethel or Aurora, there was no written creed to argue
about.

Nor did members have written deeds to their land. Until 1872, nearly all Colony land and buildings were owned by Dr. Keil in his name. But the members considered themselves part owners, since they had contributed everything they had to the Society when they joined. However, they held no legal title. It was all on faith and trust.

Members also contributed daily the products of their labor. These contributions from their farms and shops went into the common storehouse, from which members withdrew whatever they needed. No money was involved nor were records kept. What was left over was sold outside the Colony. That cash went into the treasury, which Dr. Keil looked after. This trade with nonmembers, for which records were kept, could be and indeed was called "Wm. Keil & Co." For example, that was the identification stencilled on the boxes of apples sold by the Colony.

The Aurora Colony communal storehouse, to which members contributed their products and from which they withdrew what they needed.

There were exceptions to this arrangement. Some members sold products privately to non-Colony customers. Aurora was an informal blend of communal and private economies.

But though Aurora was largely communal, Dr. Keil was nothing like a commissar running a collective farm. Rather, he was a father figure. He saw that everyone was taken care of, in old age and in sickness. He assigned jobs, sometimes approved or discouraged marriages, and generally was a patriarch looking after the Colony members, who were like a large family. This relationship was satisfactory to most of the older members. They were living well, not working very hard, enjoying many small pleasures, and the leader was doing whatever worrying needed to be done. But the younger members sometimes found Dr. Keil, in his patriarchal role, stern or meddlesome.

In April 1866, Dr. Keil drew up a written constitution for the Aurora Colony. This document purportedly transferred control of the Colony from himself to a "Board of Trustees." Apparently he took this uncharacteristic step because some members were dissatisfied with his leadership. Most members seem generally to have been content, and, for practical purposes, everything went on as before. The Trustees (appointed by Dr. Keil and serving at his pleasure) never opposed him, though they may have given him advice. No property titles were transferred to the Trustees.

The men in the Colony were busy as farmers, carpenters, cabinet makers, tailors, hatmakers, shoemakers, millers, sawyers, butchers, weavers, blacksmiths, and so on. Nearly all members' clothing, furniture, and household items were made within the Colony. And of course the men had to spend some time (enjoyably) practicing those musical instruments.

An Aurora quintet.
Left to right: Andrew Giesy, Emanual Keil, Frederick Giesy,
his son Henry, William Giesy, and Fred Will, Sr.

The women also had plenty to do. Their chores were described in a letter written by Christina Schuele Snyder (wife of Charles Snyder) in 1927, when she was 79 years old. She came to Aurora from Bethel in 1863, when she was 15 years old, and lived the rest of her life in Aurora. Here are her recollections:

> "Besides caring for her family and keeping her house, the Colony housewife's days were crowded with numerous other tasks. She was compelled to make by hand the various articles which women of today buy at stores as a matter of course. Modern machinery performs quickly the tasks over which she spent many tedious hours.

"Possibly the most important and interesting of her tasks was spinning. After the sheep was shorn, the wool was washed, carded, or picked and spliced. It was then ready for the spinning wheel. These wheels were of wood, and home-made. When the yarn was spun it was ready to be woven into garments, quilts, etc. on the hand looms. Before these were woven, the yarn was dyed. The principal colors used were black, blue, red, green, and brown. The red color was obtained from the madder root. It could be gathered at any time of year if needed. This root was cultivated in the family garden. All yarn was treated with an alum process to make colors fast. Black walnut hulls were used to dye brown. Green was obtained by boiling peach leaves.

"Lye was made by placing ashes over straw in a sort of hopper. Water was poured over this, and the fluid which seeped through was lye.

"Bones, rind, and grease of hogs were saved for soap-making. This, with the lye, was cooked in a huge kettle over an open fire.

"Tallow for candles was obtained from suet. This was melted and poured into the candle mold. The wick was, of course, placed in the center of the mold.

"Some baskets were woven of straw. The bread was set to raise in such baskets, which were shaped like mixing bowls. Other more substantial baskets were woven of split wood.

"The men of the Colony usually did the weaving."[13]

Even before October 1870 when the railroad introduced some worldly influences into Aurora, there was some restlessness and dissatisfaction, and also some apprehension that the Colony organization would not last. This is shown in a letter written by Philip Snyder to his father Michael. That Snyder family had been sent by Dr. Keil from Bethel to the Nineveh site early in 1850. They are shown at Nineveh in the U.S. Census taken in the summer of that year. Philip had come to Aurora (probably in the 1867 wagon train) but the rest of the family remained at Nineveh. Here is an abridgement of Philip's letter. In reading it, we need to judge his English style and spelling leniently, remembering that these people all spoke German in early life. They learned English initially as a second language, which gradually became their primary language.

In 1869, Philip was 29 years old and father Michael was 62.

> Aurora Mills P.O., Marion County
>
> October 31st, 1869
>
> Dear Father, Mother, Brother, and Sisters, without exception:
>
> I am not surprised if you all feel like complaining hard against me for neglecting writing to you so long.... I was with a Party sent by Doctor Keil on [to] the State Fair ground near Salem, helping to build a house to keep [a] restaurant in during the fair week, all together occupying 2 Months, [during] which time I was not at home.... Hoping these few and humble lines may find you all enjoying an all-wise, all-mighty, and all-merciful God's blessing in accordance with all your needs....

The people [here] generally enjoy usual good health.... I wish to know how you all stand about coming out here.... & I pray for brother J. Miley's full and heartfelt opinion on this particular as I do for all of yours. I for my own person believe not that I can, from free choice, stand it here longer than till Spring. I have no more the high opinion of Colony life which I had three years ago.... If I should advise you from the foundation of an honest and loveing heart, I would say make not a step to leave your old Situation; for I look for gradual dissolution here, annoyance, & trouble.... I make no secret of my intentions here. I came here with an honest intention.... While I am here I will try to compete in honest & good conduct with those who may now expect to live & die here.... If I leave here, it will be to return to you in case you all agree to stay where you are; & if I take leave from the Colony I do not expect or hope that I may be obliged to accept one cent even as a present from out of the Colony. If I did anything in the Colony to merit reward, may our Heavenly Father, when he sees fit, compensate me for it. For his word's sake alone did I do what little I have done, & through him alone can I be justified.... Margaret's and Louisa's [two of his younger sisters] letters from July 18 & 19 came to hand August the 5th, & again Louisa's from Sept. 3rd came to hand Sept. 21st.... When Louisa writes to Jonathan Novinger again she shall deliver my best regards to him and if it is so ordained I will enjoy many chats with him yet. & Margaret shall deliver my best respects to that good

Girl, Louisa Behrens, & as I am single myself
yet I would like very much to see her, & who
knows but I may, if she is not in too great a
hurry.... I send my best respects to H. Behrens & all his Folks; tell him it does me good
the present day yet to think of the simple
honest well-meant chats we had working
together.... from your sincere Son & Brother."[14]

(This is his signature   *Philip Snyder*
to the letter.)

We see that mail moved quite expeditiously between
Aurora and Nineveh in mid-1869—only 18 days! Delivery
had been accelerated in May of that year when the "golden
spike" connected the Central Pacific and Union Pacific,
establishing transcontinental rail service between San
Francisco and Omaha and the east coast. The mail traveled
by steamship between Portland and San Francisco in 1869.

The next year, Aurora's first railroad train steamed
into the Colony station for a lunch stop at the hotel. That
portentous event occurred October 4, 1870. The railroad,
the "Oregon & California," was built by Portland
promoter Ben Holladay, who had already made a fortune
with stagecoaches. In 1868, Dr. Keil had sold to Ben
Holladay a strip of land through the middle of Aurora for
the railroad right-of-way. Here was a change, indeed,
from the time, back in Bethel in 1852, when Dr. Keil had
opposed bringing the "Hannibal & St. Joseph R.R." near
his pietist utopia. But at Aurora it had apparently become
obvious that isolation was impossible, and also that
certain economic advantages came with a connection to
"the world."

Dr. Keil and Ben Holladay seem to have been compatible acquaintances. The railroad builder hired the Aurora Colony Band to promote his scheme. In 1869, he sent them on a 16-day tour to towns around Puget Sound, including Victoria, B.C. and Port Townsend. For this he paid them $500, which went into the Colony treasury.

The "O & C" received grants of government timber land to subsidize the building of the railroad. With those reserves back of him, speculator Holladay was able to sell bonds to finance construction, which began at Portland in 1868. The rails reached Salem in October 1870 and Roseburg in 1872. There, the promoters ran out of money. Despite its optimistic name, the "O & C" never reached California. It was not until 1887 that the Southern Pacific took over the "O & C" and continued the tracks over the Siskiyou Mountains. However, beginning in October 1870, the trains came to Aurora daily, and soon twice-a-day. Their schedules were arranged to provide meal stops at the already famous Aurora Colony Hotel.

1870–1877

During these latter days, most of the older Colony members remained happy and content. They had their social activities (music, dancing, festivals in the park, and the bond of friendship with kindred spirits) and also the pleasures of creating beautiful but simple furniture, hand-woven textiles, and other handicrafts.

Dr. Keil, however, suffered another blow; in 1872, his only remaining daughter, Amelia, died, probably of scarlet fever. She was 22.

Also in 1872, he transferred the title to 4,400 acres from his own name to about 150 heads of families. These were parcels they had been farming or upon which stood their homes or farmhouses. Later, he deeded more land to members until, at the time of his death in December 1877, only 2,700 acres remained in his name, out of the approximately 15,000 acres of Aurora Colony real estate. He had planned a final distribution of the land remaining in his name, but his death forestalled that.

Several factors may have prompted Dr. Keil to turn from communal to individual private ownership. The deaths of six of his children must have borne heavily upon his enthusiasm, besides reminding him grimly of his own mortality. Nor was there any possibility of a continuing "dynasty." His three remaining sons (August, Emanuel, and Frederick) had no interest in or aptitude for the kingly role. Dr. Keil had for a time hoped that Frederick, who was 27 years old in 1872, would succeed him, but Frederick was not made to be a stern autocrat. He was easy-going and gentle, though he was enough of an entrepreneur to manage the Colony's external business. Nor was Emanuel suited to such leadership, though occasionally he did lead the Aurora band. It appears that the sons were not as committed to communalism as their father.

Members were quite free to withdraw from the Aurora Society if they wished. Dr. Keil made no attempt to coerce them. According to Charles Nordhoff, who visited Aurora in 1873, Dr. Keil was wise in his dealings with dissatisfied members. "In the early days," said the Doctor, "we used sometimes to have trouble. Thus a man would say, 'I brought money into the Society and this other man brought none; why should he have as much as I?' My reply was, 'Here is your money—take it; it is not necessary; but while you remain, remember that you are no better than he.' Again, another might say, 'My labor brings one thousand dollars a year to the Society; his only two hundred and fifty.' My answer was, 'Thank God that he made you so much abler, stronger, to help your brother; but take care lest your poorer brother do not some day have to help you when you are crippled, or ill, or disabled.'"[15]

Even after the transfer of titles to individual members, the quasi-communal life of the Colony continued as before. A visitor to Aurora in 1872, Theodore Kirchhoff, left some vivid descriptions in his Memoirs. He was a California author and a writer for a German language magazine called *Gartenlaube* (Garden Bower). He traveled to Aurora with a friend, an insurance agent who hoped (he was not successful) to sell Dr. Keil life insurance policies on all his followers. Mr. Kirchhoff wrote:

"Americans called Aurora 'Dutchtown,' their generic term for German communities, used incorrectly. Reports agreed it was a model commonwealth, the best organized and most prosperous in Oregon. I heard nothing but praise for it.... As to Dr. Keil—he was the subject of the oddest rumors.... He performed marriages and was physician and midwife, preacher, secretary of state, judge, legislator, and chief executive...he answered to nobody and, by popular consent, retained the profits of everybody's labor.... Still, he accorded his subjects a good livelihood. They in turn obeyed him implicitly and revered him like a father....

"...a steam-ferry brought us from Portland across the Willamette to the Oregon & California station. Soon we were roaring south...along the majestic Willamette.... Beyond Oregon City we left the Willamette for an extensive prairie edged with forest and featuring attractive farmhouses dotted amid a scattering of groves. Then, in the distance, at the center of a prosperous settlement on portly hills and framed in green trees, the slim, white steeple of a church beckoned. We were at [Aurora]."

They went to the hotel and "assembled there with the other passengers for lunch. The 'Dutchtown' hotel...resembled a German inn of the old style. The long table and its spotless cloth groaned under a feast of German dishes excellently prepared. The waitresses were German misses, nicely dressed and attractive."

After lunch they went to Dr. Keil's house.

"From afar it resembled the house of a well-to-do German farmer. We walked there on a plank road and *en route* met and were greeted in the German way by several workers just leaving the field. They looked as if life agreed with them: young women in tucked up dresses and with rakes in hand,

Hop picking. Hops were an important crop at Aurora.

(1871) Sawyer [another judge] and I went up to Halsey and back on the railway—making near 200 miles travel in daylight.... The pleasantest part of our excursion was our supper at Dutchtown on our return. Sweet milk, apple butter, warm light biscuits and beef and potatoes fried in the old fashioned way.

(1873) Went on evening train with Mrs. D. [his wife] and Miss Lydia [Lydia Rodney] and Henders [his son Henderson] to Dutchtown. Pleasant ride and evening. At dinner had fried chicken and apple butter. Lydia was astonished and pleased with everything she saw. After breakfast walked through the orchard and park with Dr. Keil. What a wealth of fruit.... L. R. [Lydia Rodney] had become quite favorably impressed with Dr. Keil during the day.

(1874) Went to Salem.... Took an excellent dinner in great haste on the way at Dutchtown. I wish there was a Dutchtown at every station in Oregon.

(1875) Went to Aurora to attend celebration of the Fourth. Hot day.[16]

The Aurora band at an 1876 centennial celebration, with everyone in a white shirt for the occasion.

young men puffing contentedly on clay pipes. The scene was almost entirely German: pleasant, tree-shaded houses, barns, stables, and well-tended fields; gardens of flowers and vegetables; the white steeple of a church atop

The Henry Becke hophouse at Aurora.

a green hill.... We asked a friendly *hausfrau* where we might find the Doctor. 'In the orchard.'.... What a splendid orchard! Its thousands of trees were heavy with the finest fruit.... High on a ladder was the renowned Doctor, the King of Aurora, in less than regal attire (shirt sleeves, straw hat, cotton apron) picking apples. Diligently, he put the rosy-cheeked bounty into a basket. Several workers under the trees busily sorted...and carefully packed the best into boxes...."

Dr Keil gave them a guided tour of the community.

"After several hours of touring, we returned to the Doctor's residence. He invited us to a glass of homemade wine.... He served two kinds of wine: one of wild grapes, one of currants, both delicious.

"Before departing, we questioned members about the organization and government [of Aurora].... If a member leaves voluntarily, which is almost unheard of, his money is returned without interest but with a pro-rata share of the community's earnings, as determined by the Doctor. He holds the common purse. Expenses are paid out of it. Into it go the profits of the Colony's industry and agriculture. Members receive the necessities free. Whoever needs a coat or other clothing, or flour, sugar, tobacco, etc., draws from the store. Meat is likewise gratis from the butcher, and bread from the baker. Alcoholic beverages are dispensed only to the sick [but households made their own wine]. Everyone's time and talent belong to the commonwealth, subject to the judgment of the Doctor.... When a member marries, he is assigned a house and land. Families are thus scattered on farms. Elders assist the Doctor by giving aid and counsel to the exercise of his office....

"At once spiritual and temporal head, [Dr. Keil] can ordain what he pleases. Though called a communist society, Aurora is nothing but a big farm, established and run by the talented Doctor. If his power is subject to the approval of the elders, they always uphold him.... Members lead a carefree life; only the Doctor has to worry his head. Hence Aurora's placid durability... Combine his skill in organization with his unlimited power...add the assiduous effort and organized diligence of the Germans, and you have the recipe for Aurora's prosperity.... Aurora has a church and school. It takes the newspapers and buys the books that the Doctor authorizes.... There are social events as well as vocal and instrumental music. These features, together with an easily earned livelihood, satisfy the members—while the good Dr. Keil sees to everything else. Will Aurora continue after he dies? I doubt it. Nobody else enjoys the membership's trust and can lead."

Author Kirchhoff went on to call Dr. Keil "a charismatic herb and miracle healer" who became "King of Aurora." [12]

There are many references to the Aurora Hotel in Oregon archives and pioneers' reminiscences. Several are in the diary of Matthew Deady. By coincidence, he was the judge who, in 1883, approved the final disposition of Aurora property among Colony members. Here are four comments from Judge Deady's diary:

Despite the prosperity, and the contentedness of most of the older Aurorans, Dr. Keil and the elders were not able to indoctrinate all of the younger generation in the communal way of life, due to the incursion of outside and alien influences. One of these, of course, was the railroad, which brought well-dressed, relatively affluent and cosmopolitan visitors to the town and its hotel, tempting younger Aurorans with new ideas and diversions. For them, the attractions of "the world" (individual freedom and the opportunities of free enterprise and self expression) often triumphed over the monotony and collective dependence of communal living under an autocrat, however attentively benevolent.

Retrospective appraisals of Dr. Keil's character, and of the success of the Aurora Colony, are diverse and contradictory. It seems that visitors or writers with a devout Christian faith usually viewed Dr. Keil favorably, while those with a materialistic or humanistic philosophy disapproved. Perhaps the latter were unable to savor or appreciate the life-view of the Aurorans and their leader, just as Voltaire would have been an unsympathetic critic of a monastery.

Dr. Keil's health was impaired in 1877 by a heart problem and a stomach ailment, but they were not considered to be serious, certainly not critical. Nevertheless, he died suddenly December 30, 1877. For Aurora, and its parent Bethel, it was the end of what many members still regarded as their communal utopia.

Chapter 8
The End of Utopia

Because of Dr. Keil's patriarchal dominance, his death left a vacuum. Colony members felt not only bereavement but also a numbing loss of direction. If work went on, it was from the momentum of habit.

Nor was there an heir apparent to assume his role; an autocrat does not foster development of a strong successor. Dr. Keil had been well suited to "action"—migrating to the frontier and establishing a colony in a wilderness. His highly motivated, inner-directed personality was appropriate for that. But in the settled stage, for permanence, the leader must share control and prepare a successor.

If there had been enough time, Aurora might have produced such a successor. But Dr. Keil's death came too soon. He was moving in that direction—transferring ownership of properties to individual members, drawing up Articles of Agreement, and instituting a Board of Trustees (though their powers were purely nominal). Dr. Keil might have found it painful to hand over the reins—he was clearly reluctant to allow lieutenants with real authority to develop—but eventually machinery for succession might have been in place.

There were competent and well respected men in the Colony, but no one had the charisma, the magnetic personality to inspire loyal devotion among all the members, and also the desire or willingness to assume the burden of leadership. So the elders decided to dissolve the commune, and the majority of members favored that.

A few dissented. The most vocal was Christopher Wolff, who remained all his life a committed believer in communalism. In 1888, he wrote a letter containing these retrospections:

> "In Aurora lived a people that gave their property, souls and sweat to one common end: to live all alike, so there were no poor and no rich and we had a decent living too.... But it pleased the leading men to change the fundamental love, and decree that some should possess more property than others and so create poor and rich. I raised objection to this rule. Then they held a meeting...ruled me out and I was left in the cold. But I must not forget that Fred Giesy offered to pay me any sum I should name, an honorable offer, but I could not accept it, as I vowed 50 years ago, when I started from Europe, not to take any pay for my service of love, but as Christ commanded, for nothing you got it, and for nothing give it."[14]

But Professor Wolff's pietistic egalitarianism was no longer acceptable, nor was living "all alike." Such theories did not recognize the desire, especially among the younger people, for the opportunities of individualism, with scope for creativity, ambition, and enterprise.

Communalism at Aurora already had been diluted. Besides the distribution of most of the land to individual members, there were private enterprises of various kinds. For example, in the 1870s Dr. Keil's son Frederick, in partnership with F. Giesy and I. Wagner, operated a store called "F. Keil & Co." where they sold, to the general public of the region, "Dry Goods, Clothing, Boots and Shoes, Hats, Hardware, Groceries, Notions, etc."

In carrying out their decision to end the Society and to distribute the communal property to individual members, the Aurorans confronted a complex problem. The property in Dr. Keil's name at the time of his death included not only the 2,700 acres of land and some buildings at Aurora

Louisa (*nee* Reiter) Keil (1812-1879).
This photo was taken at Aurora ca. 1870,
when she would have been 58 years old.

but also properties at Bethel and Nineveh. Though the members considered all this to be communal property, it would legally have gone directly to the Keil heirs—his wife and three sons. The members held their equity on faith alone. But their faith was justified. After Dr. Keil's death, his wife and sons all signed a disclaimer to any right in the Keil properties. They agreed that Dr. Keil had held the property only in trust for the communities.

Mrs. Keil clearly understood her husband's mission. From the beginning, she had been one of his most devoted supporters. She said to Society members, "Do whatever he says; he knows everything." Louisa Keil died July 20, 1879, less than two years after her husband.

Immediately upon hearing of Dr. Keil's death, the Bethel Society sent two representatives (Jacob Miller and August Keil) to Aurora, to help settle his estate. They were in Oregon for about two months, and left Portland March 30, 1878, via steamship, for San Francisco. The *Oregonian* reported that "They have made many warm friends during their visit."

The Aurorans had some claim on a share of the properties in Missouri because they had contributed all their assets when they first joined the Bethel Society and had worked there for several years before coming to Oregon. What would be an equitable distribution among the 250 adults at Aurora and the 100 or more still at Bethel?

The Aurorans, at a general meeting in January 1879, elected three men to represent them in the negotiations: Samuel Miller, Stephen Smith, and Henry Will. The Bethelites selected five from among their members: J. G. Bauer, Philip Miller, John Shafer, Philip Steinbach, and Henry Will (not the one from Aurora, but a relative with the same name). These eight men met that spring at Bethel and, by June 1879, had made these determinations:

The Aurora school in the 1880s. Though the "colony" had ended, its life-style continued for some years.

1. The value of property in Oregon still held in Dr. Keil's name, $45,000. (This excluded the far larger portion which Dr. Keil had already distributed to individual members in 1872).

2. The value of property in Dr. Keil's name at Bethel and Nineveh, $64,000.

3. Of that total of $109,000, the Aurorans (because of their contributions and work at Bethel) were entitled to $62,000. Therefore, $17,000 should be transferred from Bethel to Aurora. So that amount of Keil property in Missouri was sold, and the proceeds were remitted to Aurora.

After that, all legal connections between Bethel and Aurora were severed. Each community then distributed the Keil assets among its members. At Aurora, those

The house of Urban and Susan Will.

Leonard Will house. His wife was Triphena Forstner.

Konrad Boehringer house.

George Kraus house.

distributions, based largely on the length of time in the Society, were allotted to the different family groups, and each of these divided its share among its members. The final distribution list was submitted to all the Aurorans for approval. No one lodged any objection. Perhaps that was a tribute not only to its fairness but also to Dr. Keil's continual preaching against "selfishness." A final decree by Judge Matthew Deady of the U.S. District Court on January 22, 1883 declared that the distribution by the trustees was "in all things ratified, confirmed, and approved."

Despite the end of the communal utopia, most Aurorans continued to live as before—in the same houses and doing the same work, though everything was now privately owned. They were all united by many years of friendship with kindred spirits, by the shared adventures, and by a simple faith. Most of the young people gradually moved to cities and some entered various professions.

A letter written at Aurora in May 1900 by Jacob Miller contains some first-hand insights into their communal experience. The letter was addressed to W. A. Hinds, who had asked some questions in connection with a book he was writing on communal societies.[17]

> "Dear Sir: I will try and answer your questions.... Bethel dissolved as a Community in 1880, and Aurora in 1881. Their dissolution was not debated before their founder's death. I think they would yet continue if he were still alive. After his death nobody fully satisfactory to the members was found willing to take the responsibility and carry the burden as leader. I am positive that a number (certainly not all) would have continued the Communities if the

right man would have been willing to take charge of them.

"In Bethel the distribution of property...was made according to the number of years each had worked in the Community....

"Of course, a few members left from time to time, but for no special reason that I know except to try individualism. Some of the young people occasionally became discontented for various causes....

"The former Community members [at Aurora] nearly all now live on the property they received in the distribution [including the earlier distributions by Dr. Keil] and I know of no one that would sell even at a good price.

"The relation between the sexes was either marriage or celibacy; a number chose the latter.

"Quite a good many of the former members still adhere to the religious doctrines held by the Community, and some few have connected themselves with the common churches.

"The opportunities at Aurora for a good common education were ample. A few of the young men developed marked ability as writers, professors of music, physicians, etc.

"Quite a number of the former members regret the dissolution of the Communities, and regard the years spent in them as the happiest of their lives....

"Dr. Keil, I think, was fore-ordained by God to fulfill a certain mission. He was the most powerful preacher I ever heard or ever expect to hear. Some persons may speak evil of him, but I revere his memory. Yours truly,

Jacob G Miller"

There were still living at Aurora, even into the 1930s, old members who had grown up in the Colony under Dr. Keil's leadership. They would often get together, and when they did there was still the bond of a great love. As one expressed it, "This love, we believe, *is* God."

Another, reminiscing about Colony days, said, *"Das war das Paradies"*—It was like Heaven!

Chapter 9
A Case History:
The Forstner Saga

In the preceding chapters, we followed the migrations of our group of pietists from Europe to Pennsylvania, Missouri, and Oregon, as seen from the viewpoint of the leaders (George Rapp and William Keil) and their objectives. But what of the individual members' hopes and fates? Some fragments of such individual histories are available, particularly for one specific family. This family participated, during a span of three generations, in all those migrations. Their chronicle and the details of their lives make the preceding generalities more personal and palpable.

In the Kingdom of Württemberg in the seventeenth century lived a family named Forstner. Their home was about 10 miles north of the city of Stuttgart, in the Enz River valley. It was a pleasant valley, with green meadows surrounded by rolling hills. On the sunny southern slopes of those hills were vineyards, and an important industry was wine-making. These inhabitants of WUrttemberg were Swabians, descendants of an ancient German tribe. The name is sometimes spelled "Suevi" or "Suebi." The Roman historian Tacitus told of them in his book *Germania*, written in A.D. 98.

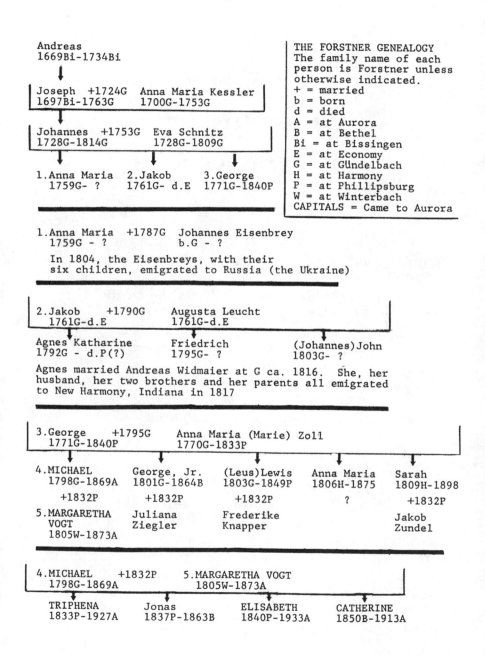

Andreas
1669Bi-1734Bi

Joseph +1724G   Anna Maria Kessler
1697Bi-1763G   1700G-1753G

Johannes +1753G   Eva Schnitz
1728G-1814G   1728G-1809G

1.Anna Maria   2.Jakob   3.George
  1759G- ?   1761G- d.E   1771G-1840P

THE FORSTNER GENEALOGY
The family name of each
person is Forstner unless
otherwise indicated.
+ = married
b = born
d = died
A = at Aurora
B = at Bethel
Bi = at Bissingen
E = at Economy
G = at Gündelbach
H = at Harmony
P = at Phillipsburg
W = at Winterbach
CAPITALS = Came to Aurora

1.Anna Maria +1787G Johannes Eisenbrey
  1759G - ?   b.G - ?

In 1804, the Eisenbreys, with their
six children, emigrated to Russia (the Ukraine)

2.Jakob   +1790G   Augusta Leucht
  1761G-d.E   1761G-d.E

Agnes Katharine   Friedrich   (Johannes)John
1792G - d.P(?)   1795G- ?   1803G- ?

Agnes married Andreas Widmaier at G ca. 1816. She, her
husband, her two brothers and her parents all emigrated
to New Harmony, Indiana in 1817

3.George   +1795G   Anna Maria (Marie) Zoll
  1771G-1840P   1770G-1833P

4.MICHAEL   George, Jr.   (Leus)Lewis   Anna Maria   Sarah
  1798G-1869A   1801G-1864B   1803G-1849P   1806H-1875   1809H-1898

+1832P   +1832P   +1832P   ?   +1832P

5.MARGARETHA   Juliana   Frederike   Jakob
  VOGT   Ziegler   Knapper   Zundel
  1805W-1873A

4.MICHAEL   +1832P   5.MARGARETHA VOGT
  1798G-1869A   1805W-1873A

TRIPHENA   Jonas   ELISABETH   CATHERINE
1833P-1927A   1837P-1863B   1840P-1933A   1850B-1913A

Joseph Forstner, son of a certain Andreas Forstner, was born in 1697 in Bissingen, a village near the point where the Enz River flows into the Neckar River. Joseph grew up as a vine dresser—one who tends grape vines— and he worked in his father's vineyard. He was following the vocation of his paternal ancestors. When he reached adulthood, Joseph moved from Bissingen to Gündelbach, another village about eight miles across the valley. We don't know why he moved, but it may well have been because of the European tradition of primogeniture, whereby the oldest son inherited all of the father's land. The purpose of that custom was to prevent a land holding from being divided among many brothers generation after generation into ever-smaller and uneconomic plots. If an elder brother was in line to inherit Andreas' family vineyard, Joseph would have had to follow a different vocation or find some land elsewhere. One way was to marry the daughter of a landowner who didn't have any sons.

At Gündelbach in 1724, Joseph, then 27 years old, married Anna Maria Kessler, who was born there in 1700. In 1728, a son was born to Joseph and Anna Maria. They named him Johannes and had him baptized in the Lutheran Church. The Lutheran Church was the estab- lished or official state church in Württemberg, because the king was Lutheran. That was the arrangement in the various German states, and there was a close connection between church and state. In Bavaria, for example, the ruler was a Roman Catholic, and so that was the state church there. All of the people—except a few persecuted nonconformists—were communicants of the same church denomination to which their king or prince belonged.

Joseph had become a "weingartner" (one who cul- tivates a vineyard) and his son Johannes became one, too. When Johannes was 25 years old, in 1753, he married Eva Schnitz, who was also 25 years old. She was a descendant of one George Schnitz, a blacksmith born in Gündelbach in 1664. In church records, Johannes is identified as *"Bürger und weingartner,"* that is, a citizen of the town and a landholder, with a vineyard which he owned and cultivated.

The character and philosophy of the typical Swabian man, in the opinion of Germans from other German states, is something like this: Work, Work, Work, Build a house, Marry, Have children, and Don't look at other women. Johannes and Eva produced nine children, but six of them died in infancy or early childhood, a heart-rending ratio which was not unusual in those days. Eva, later, became a midwife, and she certainly had had enough personal experience to qualify. Their three children who survived to adulthood were Anna Maria (born in 1759 and named, presumably, for Johannes' mother), Johannes JAKOB (born in 1761) and Johannes GEORGE (born in 1771).

The sons' names illustrate a custom often followed in Germany at that time, whereby a son would have his father's first name, plus a different middle name. He would be identified by his middle name.

The passing on of the first name was a sentimental paternal link. However, it is a great nuisance for historians, as is also the custom of naming daughters for their mothers or grandmothers. In the following pages, Johannes JAKOB will be called JAKOB, and Johannes GEORGE will be called GEORGE, as they were known in real life.

The Forstners all became disciples of George Rapp, whose career as a nonconformist evangelist was described in Chapter 4. Gündelbach, where the Forstners lived, was seven miles from Iptingen, the home of Herr Rapp, and well within the radius of his meetings and preaching. As followers of a pious separatist who was rebelling against the established church—a church closely allied to the civil authority—the Forstners were obviously not compulsively conformist or bound by convention. Already we see the Forstners as independent in spirit. It was a trait they were to reveal again from time to time.

The Forstners were among the 300 families who, by 1793, comprised preacher Rapp's "congregation." By that year there were three Forstner households: (1) George, then 22, was still living with his parents; (2) Anna Maria had married Johannes Eisenbrey; and (3) Jakob had married Augusta Leucht.

Son George had to find some other vocation than *"weingartner"* because his older brother Jakob would inherit the family vineyard. He became a carpenter. He seems to have been a good one. And his prospects were sufficiently promising for him to take a wife. In 1795, he married Anna Maria Zoll, who was born at Gündelbach in 1770. With a confusing number of the girls in this chronicle named "Anna Maria," it is fortunate that this one was generally called "Marie," and she will be so identified henceforth. Marie was from an old family thereabouts, going back in church records at least to a Paulus Zoll born there in 1583.

One would have thought that life there in the Enz Valley would have been idyllic: the neatly-cultivated fields and vineyards, the wine-making (and, surely also, the wine-drinking), and the growing families in loving homes. On the contrary, those were troublesome times, and there was a large emigration out of Württemberg. What were the problems?

The causes of unrest were complex, but they may be summarized under five headings. They all burdened or distressed the Forstner households in varying ways.

(1) Over-population. There was no land that was not already owned. Younger sons had to move into towns and

become artisans, craftsmen, or employees. Their desire to possess land and a farm remained unachievable.

(2) A static economy and a rigid class structure. There was little "upward mobility" for anyone with ambition to rise in the social scale or improve his economic fortunes.

(3) Oppressive rulers. The kings and princes of the numerous German states were notoriously autocratic. They imposed high taxes to pay for their lavish living (including their passion for the sport of hunting), which contrasted jarringly with the lot of their hardworking subjects.

(4) Military occupation. The southwestern German states lay between the often contending powers of France and Prussia. During the Seven Years War (1756-63), French troops marched back and forth through Württemberg. In 1796, Napoleon's French troops occupied Württemberg and Bavaria, living on the country's resources and imposing severe requisitioning. Occupying troops were quartered on the local homeowners. Occasionally, a German prince would find a way to retain his rule by making a compact with Napoleon whereby the prince would agree to conscript his own men to serve in Napoleon's army against the Prussians or Austrians. In 1805, a French army moved through Württemberg and in October of that year defeated an Austrian army at Ulm, an ancient Swabian city.

(5) Religious intolerance. This was a factor primarily in Württemberg, not because intolerance was more repressive there, but because the Swabians were particularly attracted to pietism and "Early Christianity." Only in Württemberg were religious reasons a major cause of emigration. There, people of all classes joined the movement of Swabian Pietism. Laymen like George Rapp expounded the Word of God, taking the Faith out of the hands of the official state-sponsored clergy. As some have expressed it, The Faith left the cold rationalist church and entered the warm home-study groups.

All of these factors, but especially the desire for religious freedom, induced the Forstners to support George Rapp's decision to emigrate. In 1803, "Father" Rapp sailed to America, taking with him money contributed by his followers to enable him to buy the property that became Harmony, Pennsylvania. The next year, George Forstner, his wife Marie, and their three young children all left Württemberg to join the Harmony Society. In a group of 269 Rappites, they sailed from Amsterdam on the *Atlantic* and arrived September 15, 1804 at Philadelphia. The three children were Michael, born in 1798; George, Jr., born in 1801; and Johan Leus or Lewis (the spelling is not clear in the hand-written records—we will call him Lewis), born in 1803. Marie must have had her hands full on that slow voyage, managing three little boys aged 6, 3, and 1.

George Forstner signed the Articles of Incorporation forming the Harmony Society in February 1805 and also the memorial to President Jefferson referred to on page 18. Here is a facsimile of his signature on the memorial. The long "s" is a characteristic of old German script. "Georg" is the proper spelling of the name in German.

It was in 1807 that Father Rapp persuaded the Harmonists to adopt celibacy as the Society's policy. By that time, George and Marie had four children, a daughter, Anna Maria (another instance of this oft-repeated name) having been born in September 1806. These Forstners, again showing a spirit of independence, were among those who disagreed with the celibacy doctrine—not only disagreed with it but ignored it. In January 1809, another daughter, Sarah, was born to them. Nevertheless, they remained in the Harmony Society.

When the Society moved to New Harmony, Indiana, in 1815, George, the carpenter, had much work to do in building the new town. His son, Michael, who was 17 years old in 1815, was by then also a carpenter like his father. The buildings at New Harmony embodied their handiwork. A map of New Harmony, with all the streets neatly laid out at right angles, shows the home of George Forstner, at the corner of Brewery and Church streets. Behind the house was a garden and also a "joiner shop" where George did carpentry and cabinet work. Living with George and Marie were their five children.

Meanwhile, back at Gündelbach, George's sister Anna Maria, with her husband Johannes Eisenbrey and their six children, had emigrated to Russia. They left in 1804, the same year George left for America. For many years, there had been emigration from Germany to Russia, dating back to the reign of Peter the Great (Czar from 1682-1725), who had been particularly interested in attracting German technicians, scientists, merchants, and military officers. This migration was accelerated by Catherine II (Empress of Russia 1762-96). She herself was a German princess who had married the Russian Czar Peter III. As she became better acquainted with him, she found him to be a dull and stupid fellow. So (according to the rumors perpetuated by historians) she poisoned him. That not only unburdened her of a tiresome affiliation but, as a sort of extra dividend, made her "Empress," since she was next in line to succeed to the throne. So successful was her rule that forever after she has been called Catherine the Great! In 1763, she issued a decree offering immigrants to Russia free land, free and unrestricted practice of their religion, control of their own schools, exemption from military service, and grants of money to help pay travel expenses. Her generous-sounding invitation (some of the promises never materialized) was accepted by thousands of Germans. Many left from the German state of Hesse, particularly from the region around Frankfurt. These went primarily to the Volga River valley in the steppes of eastern Russia. Many also went from Württemberg; most of these went to the Odessa region, that is, the Ukraine. Among these emigrants were the Eisenbreys.

Herr Eisenbrey's occupation at Gündelbach had been "gravedigger." It was a humble but perfectly respectable profession, and one which, given the mortality rate, must have provided more than occasional employment. And perhaps he was as jovial as the gravediggers in *Hamlet*. Even so, it would not have been easy for him to support his household of eight. Ambition might enable him to rise in the economic and social scale? Not easily, in an economically static and class-structured society. If one were born a gravedigger one was likely to live and die one—likely to go on digging graves until someone else (probably one of his sons who had inherited the role) had to dig one for him personally. So, why not emigrate to the Ukraine, where a new, expanding, and socially fluid environment might give scope for ambition, as well as freedom of worship.

The Eisenbreys got on a barge at Ulm, which is at the head of navigation on the Danube River. There is at Ulm a monument to the thousands of Swabians who, over many decades, emigrated to the Ukraine and other eastern regions. From Ulm, the Eisenbreys floated down the river nearly to its mouth on the Black Sea, and from there went overland to Odessa and to the German settlements in the Ukraine. There, in the vastnesses of Russia, we lose track of that branch of the Forstners. We can only hope they throve mightily.

After 1804, there remained at Gündelbach brother Jakob and his family, and the parents, Johannes and Eva. Eva died in 1809. Father Johannes, who was 81 years old when his wife died, probably moved in with son Jakob and the grandchildren. Johannes died in 1814. Three years later occurred the final exodus of the Forstners. In 1817, Jakob, his wife Augusta, and their three children, in a group of 150 Rappites, sailed across the Atlantic and joined brother George at New Harmony, Indiana. Jakob and Augusta had these children with them on that 1817 voyage: (1) Agnes Katharine, born in 1792. She had married Andreas Widmaier, a tailor, who came with them; (2) Friedrich, born in 1795; and (3) Johannes (later Anglicized to John), born in 1803. Jakob would have had no difficulty in selling the family vineyard, since land was scarce and much in demand.

George and Jakob and their families moved with Father Rapp back to Pennsylvania, to Economy, in 1824. There, again, the carpenters George and Michael had much to do, building another new town. And the younger son, George, Jr., had also by now become a carpenter. In 1824, George, Sr., was 53 years old, Michael 26, and George, Jr. 23.

In 1827, Father Rapp and his adopted son Frederick drew up new Articles for the Society's members to sign. The new contract gave increased power to the Rapps over the Society's finances and other affairs, and several families and individuals withdrew during the years 1827-29 because of those new Articles. One group of these seceders went to Ohio. In 1828, John Forstner, son of Jakob and Augusta, left the Society, and his brother Friedrich probably also withdrew at that time—we find no further references to either of them. The father, Jakob, and the mother, Augusta, evidently remained in the

Society, where they would have been cared for until they died. They were both 67 years old in 1828.

Also remaining at Economy were George, his wife Marie, and their children. In 1828, George was 57 years old and Marie 58, and their five children's ages ranged from 30 to 19. These five, like most of the other children in the Society, had grown up and reached marriageable age, but they could not marry and remain in the Society because of Father Rapp's doctrine of celibacy. Herr Rapp did his best to keep the sexes separated, but surely the young people occasionally exchanged wistful looks or tender glances. And perhaps a *fräulein* might write on a boy's slate "I love you, Joe"—except, in this case, it would have been *"Ich liebe dich, Michael."* So, with these frustrations, it's not surprising that, in 1831 when the bogus and disruptive "Count Leon" arrived, his message of "greater luxury and an end to celibacy" fell on receptive ears. Among those who left with the Count in April 1832 to form the more liberal community at Phillipsburg were George and Marie Forstner and their five children.

Marie seems to have been a prime mover in their decision to leave. Her name appears in a list published in February 1832 of those "denouncing George and Frederick Rapp." She was then 62 years old and thinking, possibly, how nice it would be to become a grandmother— something that was not going to happen at Economy.

At Phillipsburg, George and his sons had again much carpentry to do, building the houses, church, and factories of another new town. But even while the lumber was being sawed and the nails driven, several marriages took place. Four of George's children were married in the first few months.

Michael married Margaretha Vogt. The Vogts had been supporters of Father Rapp in Württemberg. They came from a village called Winterbach, a few miles east of Stuttgart, where Margaretha was born in 1805 shortly before the family emigrated to Pennsylvania. Her father, Daniel Vogt, had been one of those independent Harmonists who had continued to have children (for a total of six) after Father Rapp's ban on such goings-on.

George, Jr., married Juliana Ziegler. She was born in 1808 in a village called Weingarten, about 20 miles west of Gündelbach.

Lewis married Frederike Knapper. The Knappers had joined the Harmony Society in 1817, probably arriving with Jakob Forstner.

Magdelena (*nee* Vester) Vogt.
Born at Winterbach in 1780; died
at Phillipsburg in 1867. She was
the wife of Daniel Vogt and the
mother of Margaretha.

Margaretha (*nee* Vogt) Forstner.
Born at Winterbach in 1805; died
at Aurora in 1873. She was the
wife of Michael Forstner.

Sarah married Jakob Zundel. The Zundels came from the village of Wiernsheim, two miles from George Rapp's home at Iptingen, and arrived at the Harmony Society in August 1805. Jakob Zundel was "converted" by a Mormon missionary in 1836, with the result that Sarah spent her last years in Utah.

These families had all known each other in Württemberg as followers of George Rapp, and the children had grown up together in the Society, so the marriages, though prompt, were not impetuous or ill-considered.

Also among those who withdrew to Phillipsburg in 1832 was Jakob's daughter Agnes Katharine, her husband Andreas Widmaier, and their children. We don't know what became of Agnes and her family or of her brothers Friedrich and John. Thus the Jakob Forstner family fades from our saga, its members disappearing into the expanding and dynamic American society.

It is pleasant to record that mother Marie Forstner was able to see, before she died November 20, 1833, one grandchild: Triphena, born to Michael and Margaretha September 4, 1833. Marie's husband, George, had been made a grandfather at least seven more times before he died at Phillipsburg in 1840.

The group who seceded with Count Leon in April 1832 numbered 176, so there were many other marriages besides those of the four Forstner children. Father Rapp was deeply saddened by the departure of "his most promising young people." Poor Father Rapp!—trying so hard to follow the Word of God as he understood it, but walking a path that was beginning to look like a dead end, as he presided over a moribund Society that slowly turned into an old folks' home.

Count Leon left (or fled?) in the summer of 1833 and the communal society at Phillipsburg was dissolved in August of that year. Everything was divided among the residents, and all property was owned privately. "Phillipsburg" ceased to exist in any legal sense; it was merely a collection of houses and buildings. In January 1841, the residents, among whom the Forstners were active, petitioned to incorporate the community as "The Town of Phillipsburg." The signatures of Michael, George, Jr., and Lewis (or Leus) appear on the legal papers incorporating the town.

Into this little community of Swabian pietists and now unattached utopians came, about the year 1840 or 1841, William Keil, preaching a doctrine of communal living, at a site "somewhere out west." The Forstners had not forgotten their dream, that elusive ideal Christian utopia, and they became disciples of Dr. Keil.

The Michael Forstner family joined Dr. Keil at Bethel in 1845. Since Phillipsburg was on the bank of the Ohio River, riverboats to Hannibal would have been conveniently accessible. At Bethel, carpenter Michael's handiwork was embodied in the elegant church and the "Elim" mansion described in Chapter 5. His daughter Catherine (known in the family as "Kathy") was born at Bethel February 13, 1850.

Brother Lewis died at Phillipsburg in 1849, so he and his family diverge from this saga of Bethel and Aurora. Brother George remained at Phillipsburg for several years, working as a carpenter, not in a utopian commune but in a "private enterprise" economy. He and Juliana had seven children, all born at Phillipsburg from 1834 to 1848. Then, probably because of letters from brother Michael extolling Dr. Keil's communal society, George and his family moved to Bethel. That was about 1849. They were certainly there by the summer of 1850; the 1850 federal census for Bethel lists Michael Forstner, occupation "millwright," and George Forstner, carpenter.

Michael by then was 52 years old and George 49, both young and vigorous enough to add their experience to the development of Bethel. They were among Dr. Keil's key men. In a list of former Harmony and Economy members, obtained from the records of the Bethel Society and said to include some of the "most valuable men" at Bethel, are these names (arranged alphabetically—no intimations of relative worth in the sequence): John Bauer, George Forstner, Michael Forstner, Adam Keller, Christian Schmidt, George Schnaufer, Samuel Schreiber, Adam Schuele, Mattheus Schuele, Jacob Vaihinger, David Wagner, and George Ziegler.

None of the Forstners accompanied Dr. Keil on the first wagon train to Oregon in 1855. If they had an

Catherine Forstner.
She was born at Bethel in 1850, and died at Aurora in 1913.
This tintype was taken at Bethel in 1860.

inclination to move to Oregon at that time, they resisted it, while waiting for more information—a wise decision, considering the difficulties and discomfort at Willapa and during the first year or two at Portland and Aurora. But at least two Forstners were among the 252 Bethelites in the 1863 train led by Christopher Wolff. One was Michael's daughter Triphena (born at Phillipsburg in 1833) with her husband Leonard Will and their six-month-old, Leonard, Jr. The other was George's oldest son, Benjamin. After only two years in Dr. Keil's Aurora community, Benjamin withdrew and moved to Salem. There he became a gunsmith and also an inventor, patenting a new type of drill known as the "Forstner bit."

Among the personal letters written by and to Forstners is one from Jonas Forstner, written May 28, 1863, to friends and relatives in the 1863 wagon train. He had just received a letter from St. Joseph, reporting on the progress of the wagon train to that point. Jonas was Michael's son, born at Phillipsburg in 1837. He was in poor health, and died at the age of 26 in December 1863, about six months after he wrote this letter. Half of the letter is in English and half in German (or rather, "Pennsylvania Deutsch"). He and all of the Bethelites and Aurorans were in a transitional stage between German and English at this time. The first part of the letter, to his cousin George Wolfer, was in English, but an English which shows his German background. Here are some portions of it:[14]

> ...I will take my pen in hand to let you know that I receift your letter from St. Joe, and it pleast me very well that you thought of me.... I hope these few lines will find you all well and healthy.... Dear George, I wish I could camp a night with you to see how the camping goes on the plains. I think it goes fine. I think often

Jonas Forstner was born in Phillipsburg in 1837, and died at Bethel in 1863, at the age of 26, after an extended illness. This tintype was taken at Bethel ca. 1860–62.

about you and Samuel and the others which
are along.... Only a lonesome time sinse you
left us. You can't see so many boys standing
on the street as before, and Sundays in the
meeting you could see how many left us—you
could get a bench alone to sit in.... I am working in the shop making spinning wheels as
much as I can do.... I think it will be peace by
you the whole journey. And I wish I was along
with you, for I think I would get well making
such a trip. But now I am not, so I must close
my writings for this time. And don't forget
me, George. I will give my best respects to you
and to Samuel Wolfer and to the Whole family. And father and mother [Michael and Mar-
garetha] give their best respects to your
Father and Mother and to the whole family.
And Elisabeth [his sister] gives her best
respects to you and Samuel and to J. Fisher
and G. Krause.

The second half of the letter, in German, was
addressed to his brother-in-law, Leonard Will. Here is a
translation and paraphrase:

We have not forgotten you and are thinking about you every day. We wish we could
spend a few hours with you and see how the
little Leonard [aged 6 months] likes it; I'm
sure he likes it fine.... I am working in the
shop as much as I am able to. I wish that I
were healthier and could make a lot of spinning wheels because there is so much
demand for them and no one here to build
them. I hope that I shall feel well again
soon....I hope you won't forget, when you have

the opportunity, to write to us. Greetings to you and to Triphena [his sister] from me and all of us. And a special greeting to Captain Wolff from me.

Jonas Forstner

(This is his signature on that letter.)

Michael and Margaretha Forstner and their two remaining children. Elisabeth and Catherine, came to Aurora on the third wagon train, in 1865. This group of 80 people was led by John Vogt, who was Margaretha's brother.

George Forstner, Jr. died at Bethel August 13, 1864, aged 63. His daughter Sophia married John Bier, in November 1861. His daughter Rosine (or Rosa) married August Keil, in January 1864. August, the oldest surviving son of Dr. Keil, had been sent from Aurora back to Bethel to act as his father's viceroy.

The Forstners enjoyed penmanship, as we saw from Jonas' flourished signature. There also survives a copybook (a bound volume of lined blank paper) which belonged to Catherine Forstner, containing many pages of her precise handwriting. She copied, in carefully shaded pen-and-ink letters, poems and also the words of songs she liked, many having the sentimental flavor characteristic of the nineteenth century. Some are in German and some in English. Her script is old-fashioned German Gothic—beautiful, but difficult to read today, even for those fluent in German. Her first entry in that copybook was a poem, in German, which may well have had special

Michael Forstner, a carpenter at five successive communes. He was born at Gündelbach in 1798 and died at Aurora in 1869. He, his wife Margaretha, and his daughters Elisabeth and Catherine came from Bethel to Aurora in 1865.

Elisabeth Forstner.

She was born at Phillipsburg in 1840 and died at Aurora in 1933. This picture was taken about 1880. She was wearing a dress and blouse she made.

Catherine Forstner at about the time she made the covered-wagon trip to Aurora in 1865 (when she was 15 years old) or shortly thereafter. She later married Henry Snyder, Jr.

meaning to her, as she crossed the plains in a covered wagon at the age of 15. Here is a translation and paraphrase of it:

The roses were just blooming when I went away;
The larks were singing their morning song.
I have to go, I have to go even farther away.
I must go even farther and farther away.
And I looked from the mountain back again at my homeland.
The bells of the herds in the quiet valley spoke
        to me for the last time.
May God put his fatherly hands over my homeland.
And farther and farther my fate calls me, but I don't
        find the happiness of my homeland.

Michael died at Aurora in 1869, and Margaretha in 1873. Daughter Elisabeth did not marry, but she became a famous cook at the Aurora Hotel described in Chapter 7. Catherine married Henry Snyder and they had five children, all but one of whom left Aurora, to be absorbed in secular society. The bones of all these Forstners are buried in the Aurora Cemetery, separated from Swabia and their fatherland by thousands of miles of sailing ship, riverboat, and covered-wagon journeys, and many a long day of hard (but hopefully satisfying) work; and days also of small joys and pleasures and that Christian Love they sought in their utopia.

The Aurora Colony house of Henry Snyder, Jr., on his farm.

Catherine (*nee* Forstner) Snyder, Henry Snyder, Jr., and their five children: Emma, Tobias, Edmund, Julius, and John. All of their clothes, including their shoes, were home-made. This photograph was taken ca. 1892.

Postscript and
Acknowledgments

The pleasure of putting together this history of the Aurorans was only slightly diminished by the frustrating inadequacy of reliable source material. Not that there is any lack of "stories" about Aurora. But many of them are second-hand creations derived from previous stories which, in turn, were based on conflicting recollections many years after the event, sometimes imaginatively embellished. There are gross inconsistencies and unfillable gaps, among which the wary historian must grope his way with care.

The problem arises because neither Dr. Keil nor his followers cared much for written records. As one Colony descendant (my father, as it happens) told me years ago when I began some Auroran genealogical research, "In the old days, no records were kept. It was sufficient that each person knew he had been born. No one felt any need to put it down on paper."

Despite that difficulty, this present volume is, I hope and believe, factual. In making it so, I was encouraged by many Colony descendants, and I also received substantial help from Patrick Harris, director of the Old Aurora Colony Museum. The archival material at the Museum's library has been indispensable. The details of the distribution of Colony property, in Chapter 8, are drawn largely from primary research done by Alan Yoder, a

Colony descendant and formerly on the staff of the Aurora Colony Museum. However, the text of this book, as to both style and content, and the judgments about what to include in it, are my own responsibility.

All of the photographs in Chapters 1 through 8 are from the archives of the Aurora Colony Historical Society, and are reproduced by permission. Those in Chapter 9 are private heirlooms.

The calligraphed maps were done by Katherine Cameron.

The photograph of the author, on the back cover, was taken by Grace Pitzer.

The cover, showing the Aurora Colony Hotel in the 1870s, is a watercolor (based on historic photographs) done specially for this book by Oregon artist Clive Davies.

Eugene Snyder

Memorial Day, 1993

Notes and References

1. Lockwood, George, *The New Harmony Movement.* New York: 1905, p. 18.

2. Ibid., p. 30.

3. Ibid., p. 10.

4. *Missouri Historical Review.* January 1974, pp. 225-231. This is a letter written by one Wilhelm Weitling in May 1852 immediately after he had visited Bethel.

5. Ibid., p. 229.

6. Ibid., p. 320.

7. Dr. Keil wrote several letters to Bethel in 1855 while he was crossing the Oregon Trail and after he reached the west coast, copies of which are in the archives of the Aurora Colony Historical Society. The excerpts reproduced here are paraphrased translations from the originals, which he wrote in German.

8. An oft-repeated guess as to the number of people in the 1855 wagon train is "175." That number (perpetuated in various articles) was based on a rough estimate of the number of wagons (35) multiplied by five, the assumed number of people per wagon. But "175" appears to be excessive; "about 150" is probably closer to the fact, and even that may be high.

9. Moss, Sydney. *Pictures of pioneer times at Oregon City, 1878* (BancMss P-A 52). Bancroft Library, University of California, Berkeley. By permission.

10. Nordhoff, Charles. *The Communist Societies of the United States*. NewYork: 1875, p. 319.

11. George Wolfer diary, in Aurora Colony Historical Society archives.

12. Kirchhoff, Theodor. *Oregon East, Oregon West, 1863-1872*. Portland: Oregon Historical Society Press, 1987, pp. 115-125.

13. Aurora Colony Historical Society archives. (Christina Schuele was born January 27, 1848.)

14. Aurora Colony Historical Society archives.

15. Nordhoff, op. cit., p. 314.

16. Deady, Matthew, Diaries. Edited by Malcolm Clark, Jr., published under title *Pharisee Among Philistines*. Portland: Oregon Historical Society Press, 1975.

17. Hinds, William A. *American Communities*. Rev. Ed. Chicago: 1908, pp. 337-9.

Bibliography

Sources cited under "Notes and References" are not included here.

Ahlstrom, Sydney. *A Religious History of the American People*. Yale University, 1972.

Arndt, Karl. *George Rapp's Harmony Society*. Associated University Press, Rev. Ed., 1972.

Barthel, Diane. *Amana*. University of Nebraska Press, 1984.

Becker, Carl. *The Heavenly City of the Eighteenth Century Philosophers*. 1932.

Bek, William. "The Community at Bethel, Missouri, and Its Offspring at Aurora, Oregon." *German American Annals*, vol. 7, Sept-Dec. 1909.

Bestor, Arthur. *Backwoods Utopias*. University of Pennsylvania, 1970,

Calverton, V. F. *Where Angels Dared to Tread*. Bobbs-Merrill, 1941.

Cross, Whitney. *The Burned-Over District: The Social and Intellectual History of Enthusiastic Religion in Western N.Y., 1800-1850*. Cornell University, 1950.

Finck, Henry T. *My Adventures in the Golden Age of Music*. New York, 1926, pp. 1-40.

Hendricks, Robert. *Bethel and Aurora*. New York, 1933.

Johnson, Paul. *A History of Christianity*. 1976.

Lyman, H. S. "The Aurora Community." *Oregon Historical Quarterly*, vol. 2, (1901), pp. 78-93.

Olsen, Deborah. "Musical Heritage of the Aurora Colony." *Oregon Historical Quarterly*, vol. 79 (1978), pp. 233-267.

Reinhardt, Kurt. *Germany: 2000 Years*. Rev. Ed. New York, 1961.

Index

A

Amana Society, 4
Atlantic, sailing ship, 17
Aurora Colony: Name,
  63; Constuction, 63–64;
  Dress, 5; Band, 68, 74,
  94; Hotel, 74, 87, 90;
  Church, 75–77; Park
  House, 75; Railroad,
  86–87, 89; Legal
  Dissolution, 104

B

Bauer, John G., 100, 121
Becke, Henry, 91
Behrens, H., 86
Behrens, Louisa, 86
Bethel Society: Name,
  33; Population, 34, 36;
  Contract Provisions,
  34–36; Buildings, 37–
  39; Products, 41–43
Bier, John, 126
Boehringer, Konrad, 103

C

Canton, sailing ship, 17
Count Leon, 25–27

D

Deady, Matthew, 93–94,
  104

E

Economy Society, 25–28
Elim, 37

F

Finck, Henry C., 66, 75,
  78
Finck, Henry T., 75
Fisher, J., 125
Forstner, Benjamin, 123
Forstner, Catherine.
  See Catherine Forstner
  Snyder
Forstner, Elisabeth,
  126, 128, 130
Forstner, George, Sr.,
  110–11, 113–14, 116–17
Forstner, George, Jr.,
  113, 116, 118, 120–21,
  126
Forstner, Jonas, 123–
  126
Forstner, Margaretha,
  119, 126, 130

Forstner, Michael, 113–
14, 116–17, 120–21,
126–27, 130
Forstner, Rosina, 72,
126
Forstner, Triphena, 102,
120, 123, 126
Fry, Henry, 72

G

Giesy, Andrew: Family,
29
Giesy, Andrew, Jr., 54,
72, 82
Giesy, Christian, 50, 60–
61
Giesy, Fred, 68, 82, 98
Giesy, Jacob, 5
Giesy, William, 82
Ginger, John, 50

H

Haller, Dr. Friedrich, 17
Harmony Society:
History, 17–22;
Contract Provisions, 17;
Celibacy, 20–21; New
Harmony, Indiana, 22–24
Holladay, Ben, 86, 87

K

Keil, Amelia, 73, 87
Keil, August, 8, 72, 88,
100, 126

Keil, Aurora, 69–70
Keil, Elias, 69
Keil, Emanual, 68, 73,
82, 88
Keil, Frederick, 73, 88, 98
Keil, Glorianda, 69
Keil, Louisa (daughter
of Dr. Keil), 69
Keil, Louisa Reiter (wife
of Dr. Keil), 8, 40, 99–
100
Keil, Dr. William:
Biography, 7–10, 41;
Preacher in Pittsburgh,
29; Sermons, 40;
Musician, 68; Death of
his children, 69, 71;
Photographs, 52, 71;
Colony Ruler, 81;
Death, 95, 97
Keil, Willie, 8, 53, 61
Keller, Adam, 121
Kirchhoff, Theodore, 89–93
Klein, Peter, 52
Knight, Adam, 50–51
Knight, Joseph, 50–51
Kraus, George, 103, 125

L

Link, George, 58, 77

M

Margaret, sailing ship,
17

Miller, Jacob, 100, 104–5
Miller, Phillip, 100
Miller, Samuel, 100
Moss, Sydney, 66

N

Nast, William, 9
Ninevah, Missouri, 43–44
Novinger, Jonathan, 85

O

Oregon Trail, 50, 52, 54–59, 72
Owen, Robert, 24

P

Pennsylvania "Dutch", 2
Phillipsburg, 27
Pittsburgh: Description, 30
Presser, Christian, 30

R

Rapp, George, 10, 13, 15–19
Reichert, Frederick, 22–23, 25
Rodney, Lydia, 94
Ruge, Karl, 58, 68, 73, 78–79

S

Schaeffer, Michael, 50
Schmidt, Christian, 121

Schnauffer, George, 121
Schreiber, Samuel, 121
Schuele, Adam, 29, 50, 121
Schuele, Mattheus, 121
Shafer, John, 100
Smith, David, 62
Smith, Stephen, 100
Snyder, Catherine Forstner, 121–22, 126, 129–31
Snyder, Charles, 82
Snyder, Christina, 82
Snyder, Edmund, 131
Snyder, Emma, 131
Snyder, Henry, Jr., 131
Snyder, Julius, 131
Snyder, Michael, 84
Snyder, Philip, 84–86
Stauffer, John, 50, 77
Stauffer, Stans, 50
Steinbach, Philip, 100
Swabians, 13, 107

U

United Brethren, 16

V

Vaihinger, Jacob, 121
Vogt, John, 77, 126

W

Wagner, David, 30, 121
Wagner, I., 98

White, George, 62
Will, Fred, 82
Will, Henry, 100
Will, Leonard, 102, 123,
    125
Will, Susan, 102
Will, Urban, 102
Willapa, 51
Wolfer, George, 67, 72,
    123
Wolfer, John, 69
Wolfer, Samuel, 125
Wolff, Christopher, 73,
    78, 98, 126
Württemberg, 2

Z

Ziegler, George, 72, 121
Zoar Society, 4